CROWOOD EQUESTRIAN GUIDES

Clipping, Trimming and Plaiting

JAYNE ASH

The Crowood Press

First published in 1995 by
The Crowood Press Ltd
Ramsbury, Marlborough
Wiltshire SN8 2HR

British Library Cataloguing-in-Publication Data
A catalogue record for this book is available from the British
Library.

ISBN 1 85223 907 7

Picture Credits
All photographs by the author
Line-drawings by Becky Owens

Acknowledgements
Many thanks to Susan Cox and Wendy King for their help with the
photography.

Throughout this book, 'he', 'him' and 'his' have been used as
neutral pronouns and as such refer to both males and females. The
term 'horses' may also include ponies and vice versa.

Typeset by Phoenix Typesetting, Ilkley, West Yorkshire.
Printed and bound in Great Britain by
WBC Book Manufacturers, Mid Glamorgan

Thorough grooming, clipping, trimming and plaiting can produce a really professional finish that will not look out of place in the best of show rings.

Presenting a horse to look his best is an art that may take months, if not years to perfect. Correct turnout can make even the most ordinary horse stand out from the crowd, yet the good thing is that it doesn't cost a lot of money to accomplish, just a bit of effort on your part. In addition, correct grooming and tidying not only makes your horse look nice, it also helps to keep him in good general health, so it is a necessity as much as a nicety.

The basic requirement of any well presented horse is good health and condition. Such a horse will shine naturally, and look alert and full of the joys of life; with the added benefit of thorough grooming, clipping, trimming and plaiting, a really professional finish can be achieved that will not look out of place in the most prestigious of show rings. However, correct turnout matters in *all* areas of equestrianism, not just showing, so it is something that you should aim to achieve from the outset: pride in your own and your horse's appearance is most important, as nothing looks worse than a grubby horse and a shabby rider trotting along the roads; when out with your horse you should always make a good impression. In competition it may make the difference between winning and losing, but the really important thing is that wherever you are, *you* will know your horse is something to be proud of and this will boost your confidence considerably.

The secret is to emphasize your horse's good points and disguise his bad ones. With a little knowledge and a few 'tricks of the trade' this is perfectly possible. You will never be able to 'put in what God left out' in the way of conformation and movement, but if you pay attention to detail and give those vital finishing touches it will make all the difference to your horse's appeal. One problem you may face is that it is often hard to come by this 'inside knowledge', as those who have it tend not to part with it freely. The purpose of this book therefore is to guide you through all the different areas of horse turnout, providing tips and step-by-step techniques on grooming, bathing, trimming, pulling and plaiting manes and tails, and clipping. Having followed the advice given, the only thing you will need to complete your turnout is a nice big smile, and this will arise easily from the many compliments you will receive as a result of all your hard work.

The only thing you will need to complete your turnout is a nice big smile!

YOUR HORSE'S COAT

Nearly all the horse's body is covered with hairs which are being shed and replaced by new ones all the time. These hairs grow from follicles within the outer layer of the skin which also contains sweat and sebaceous glands, nerves, tiny muscles and pigment which assigns the skin its colour. The sebaceous glands are tiny sacs connected to the hair follicles; these sacs produce an oil which helps keep the coat waterproof and the hairs pliable. Twice a year the horse moults, changing his entire coat.

The horse's coat is divided into various types of hair:

Ordinary hairs are those which cover most of the body. They carry pigment which gives the horse's coat its colour.
Tactile hairs help to protect sensitive areas such as the nostrils, ears, eyes and around the lips.
The mane and tail are made from long, coarse 'guard' hairs which are continually growing.

Cross-section of skin and hair components.

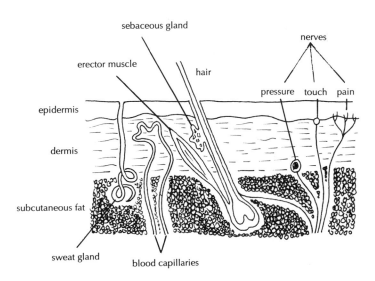

Feathers are the long hairs seen at the back of the fetlock which are only usually grown for the winter coat (at least, they are far longer and thicker at this time of the year).
Hooves are, in fact, modified hair which gives protection to the softer parts of the foot.

Horses that are exposed to cold, wet and windy weather will develop a thick winter coat made up of an inner insulating layer of soft hairs and an outer layer of coarse 'guard' hairs. Together with a layer of oil secreted from the sebaceous glands, these hair layers provide a buffer against the worst of winter weather. If your horse lives mostly outdoors, you can see why you would be doing him no favours by scrupulously grooming him with a soft brush during the winter months, as this will remove his coat oil and consequently his natural weather shield. Therefore knowing when *not* to groom your horse is often as important as correct grooming at the appropriate time.

Close-up view of a long, wet winter coat, showing how it stands erect in order to trap an insulating layer of air.

Whorls

Whorls are where the hair changes direction; they can be sited over different parts of the body, but are usually found on the chest, crest, face and flanks. They are often considered to be of little importance, but they do have a role of their own to play, in directing streams of water away from thin-skinned and sparsely haired areas of the body, down to the ground. The mane, tail and fetlocks also serve a similar purpose. Defective whorls can actually prevent a horse from thriving in the wild because he becomes wet in these sensitive areas under the belly and between the legs, and thus catches a chill.

Winter and Summer Care

The time of year will dictate the way in which you look after your horse's coat. While too much brushing of a thick winter coat can be harmful, it does still need some attention. The act of brushing stimulates the sebaceous glands to produce more oil, so a brisk brush over with a dandy brush will help to make the coat more waterproof, which in turn helps to fend off skin diseases such as mud fever and rain scald. In addition to this layer of oil keeping the horse waterproof, his coat hair must also keep him warm if he is to thrive, and in order to do this most effectively the coat hairs must trap a layer of air next to the skin, thus helping to prevent heat loss. This is achieved by a reaction similar to 'goose pimples' in humans: when the horse feels cold, tiny muscles that are attached to the hair follicles contract, thus erecting the coat hair. This allows the necessary insulating layer of air to be trapped next to the skin, and so the horse keeps warm.

In the summer the horse has the opposite dilemma, in that he needs to keep cool. In order to do so he first sheds his thick winter coat, and it is replaced by a much finer one, which facilitates the evaporation of sweat away from the body; in this way the horse can regulate his body temperature during hot spells.

GROOMING

As we have seen, the horse's coat is extremely important to his well-being, and so we do need to look after it properly and appropriately for the time of year. Many people think of grooming as a necessary chore, yet it need not be; in fact it can be an extremely pleasurable activity for both you and your horse. Your horse benefits by getting a massage, and *you* benefit by having *your* muscles toned up; not to mention the satisfaction to be gained from seeing your horse shine! The one drawback is that thorough grooming can take up quite a lot of time, usually anything upwards of an hour, so it is not something most of us can do properly each day. This will not harm the horse on a day-to-day basis as long as we always remove any mud and dirt before a ride and any sweat after a ride, but we should really put some time aside at least once a week to pay attention to this important aspect of our horse's everyday management.

Without correct grooming, your horse's coat and skin may start to suffer and you certainly won't win any prizes in the show ring. A good grooming (known as strapping) helps to massage the horse and so improve circulation. If you intend to give your horse a thorough groom, take him for an active ride beforehand so that you open up his pores and get all his natural coat oils warm. Then gather your grooming kit, making sure you have all the necessary items to hand; it is a good idea to keep them all together in a box, or grooming tray. Having everything you require in one place will prevent the need to leave your horse in the middle of a grooming session in search of a missing item, during which time he might become bored and get up to mischief.

The Grooming Kit

There are various items that make up a complete grooming kit. These are:

Body brush   This removes dust and scurf from the coat and mane and tail. It also encourages the production of oil from the sebaceous glands (*see* above, 'Winter and Summer Care').

Metal curry comb   This is used *solely* to clean the body brush. It is never used on the coat.

Dandy brush   This removes caked-on mud or dried sweat from the coat. As its bristles are fairly hard, it should not be used on horses with fine coats or those that have been clipped, or on manes or tails as it will rip the hairs.

Plastic curry comb   This is used to remove caked mud from horses that have had a good roll when out in the field. It should not be used on manes or tails, as again it will rip the hairs.

Rubber curry comb   This loosens and removes hair during moulting; it can also help to remove caked-on mud from the finer-coated horse as it is less 'prickly' than a plastic one.

Hoof pick   This cleans out the hooves.

Hoof oil   This is painted on to make the hooves shiny once cleaned.

Mane and tail comb   This is used in the process of pulling manes and tails. It should not be employed to comb the tail on a daily basis as it will pull out too many hairs, making the tail thin and wispy. However, once the mane has been brushed with a body brush, it can be used to 'lay' the mane flat.

Water brush   Use this brush to lay the mane and tail, and also to clean the feet, once picked out.

Sponges   Two of these are needed: one for the eyes and nostrils, and one for the dock.

Items in a full grooming kit.

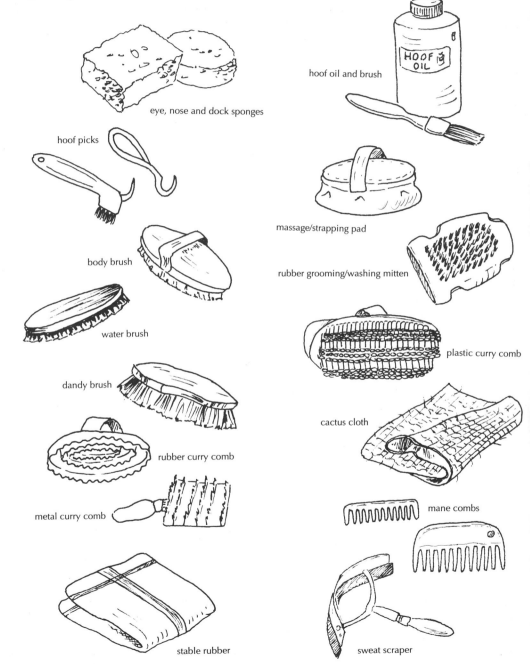

eye, nose and dock sponges

hoof oil and brush

hoof picks

massage/strapping pad

body brush

rubber grooming/washing mitten

water brush

plastic curry comb

dandy brush

cactus cloth

rubber curry comb

metal curry comb

mane combs

stable rubber

sweat scraper

Stable rubber   This removes any top dust that has settled on the coat after brushing. If used fairly vigorously it will help to massage the horse and promote distribution of the natural coat oils.

Cactus cloth   This helps to remove dried sweat and stubborn mud spots from the finer-coated horse.

Wisp   Use this as a massage aid, to help promote circulation and the distribution of coat oils.

Strapping pad   This is an alternative to the wisp.

Sweat scraper   This removes water from the coat after bathing, or after sponging down a sweaty horse.

Bucket   This holds the water needed for sponging, or you can collect the dirt in it when picking out the feet.

TYPES OF 'GROOM'

There are various ways to groom a horse, depending on the time of day and what you are about to do with him. Before riding in the mornings it is customary to give him just a quick groom; this is known as **quartering,** when you make him clean and tidy before your ride. If your horse is stabled and rugged up you do not remove his rugs but simply fold them backwards over the quarters in order to groom the forehand, and then forwards over the forehand in order to groom the quarters. Your aim is simply to give him a quick brush over in order to remove any bedding or stable stains. The mane and tail are brushed, and the eyes and dock sponged down; lastly the feet are picked out. Your horse is now ready for tacking up.

In the evenings a similar procedure is followed, when the horse is made comfortable for the night. This is known as **setting-fair.**

Giving your horse a complete groom is known as a **full groom.** Ideally this is carried out every day, but often there is insufficient time, as other tasks such as feeding and making sure the bed is clean take preference. In such cases this procedure is usually undertaken once a week.

Strapping is the name given to a grooming massage. It is usually carried out after a full groom, when the muscles are warm and relaxed. A wisp or a strapping pad is used to tone and massage the main superficial muscles. The idea is to use enough pressure so the horse holds his muscles tense for a few seconds and then relaxes. If you use the pad or wisp in a rhythmic slapping motion the horse learns to anticipate the moment of contact and thus tenses his muscles, preventing the need to slap him hard, which is incorrect although sadly

BEFORE STARTING TO GROOM, MAKE SURE THAT:

• The floor surface is neither dirty nor slippery. It is sensible to clear away bedding from the working area so that it can be swept clean of hoof pickings and other debris at the end of the session.
• You have all the necessary equipment to hand.
• Your horse is secure.

Areas of muscle which can be
toned up by wisping or
'strapping'.

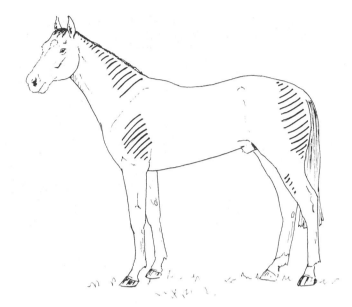

often seen. On no account do you need to whack the horse sharply,
as this will merely serve to make him apprehensive. Apply the pad
only to the main superficial areas as shown in the diagram above,
being careful not to use it over prominent bones otherwise you will
cause bruising.

Most grooming sessions will take place in the stable, although
some prefer to groom their horses outside in the yard, especially if
they are intending to bath the horse. In either case the horse must be
made secure, either by tying him up or, preferably, having someone
to hold him.

STEP-BY-STEP GROOMING TECHNIQUES

The Hooves

1. Start by picking out your horse's feet into a bucket or skip so
that you avoid making the work area messy. Use the hoof pick from
heel to toe, and ensure you get all the mud and dirt out from the
crevices around the frog.

2. Brush the hooves off with a stiff dandy brush (an old one, not
the one used for the coat) and then hose them for a few minutes. This

will help to clean them, and it will also provide moisture, which when absorbed can be beneficial if the weather is dry, or if the horse is bedded on wood chippings. Having wetted the hooves, dry the heels with a towel, to prevent the possibility of cracked heels. Once the surface of the hoof is dry, apply a coat of hoof dressing as this will help to lock in the moisture that you have provided. It is not a good idea to apply hoof dressing without hosing or tubbing the hooves first, as although it will prevent any moisture from getting out, it will also prevent any from getting in! Many people apply the hoof dressing last when grooming their horse, but this does not give it time to soak in before the horse is turned out into the paddock or put back into the stable.

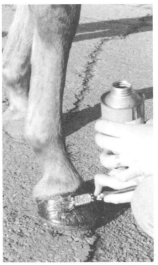

Apply a good hoof dressing and allow plenty of time for it to soak in before turning your horse out, or putting him back into his stable.

First use a dandy brush to remove any mud, and always stand to the side when attending to the hind legs.

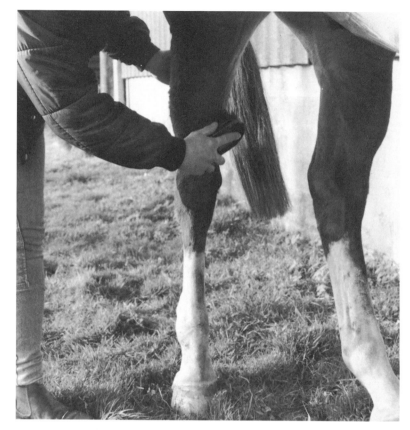

The Coat

3.   When grooming the horse, first use a dandy brush to remove any mud. Follow the lie of the coat in long sweeping movements, although it may be necessary to flick the brush outwards for a few strokes when removing a particularly stubborn patch of dried mud. Remember when brushing inside the legs to stand to the side to avoid being kicked. If your horse lives out during the winter the dandy brush is the only one you should use on his coat, otherwise you will remove the natural oils which keep him warm and healthy and his coat waterproof. For the finer-coated horse you may find a cactus cloth helpful, especially if he seems a little ticklish.

4.   Next use the body brush. Start at the head, and always work from the front backwards so that you are constantly brushing off dirt that has resettled. Untie your horse and put the headcollar around

When grooming with a body brush always hold the brush in the hand closest to your horse, so that you can put a good deal of weight behind each stroke.

his neck. Be gentle as you brush around the eyes and ears, and don't forget to talk to him to reassure him. Always try to stand slightly to the side, so that if he snatches his head up he doesn't hit you in the face; in any case you should put your hand on his nose to act as a steadying influence. When you have done the head, retie him and move on to his neck and body; over these large areas you should use firm and even pressure in a rhythmic motion. Always hold the brush in the hand nearest to your horse, so that you can put a good deal of weight behind each stroke. If you are doing it properly you should be working up quite a sweat yourself!

5. Make sure that after every few strokes you clean the body brush with the curry comb, otherwise you will find you are putting all the dust and grease back onto your horse.

6. Work all the way down each leg, until finally every part of your horse's coat has been covered.

Once you have finished this grooming routine you should be able to see a great improvement in the sheen of your horse's coat altogether, unless of course it is winter and the hair is very shaggy.

Remember to clean the body brush after every few strokes.

Manes and Tails

7.   Next, brush out the top of your horse's tail and put on a tail bandage; this will help to make it lie flat while you are getting to grips with the knots in the bottom!

8.   Take the tail in small sections. Hold the majority of the tail and let out a few strands at a time, brushing as you go, until all the tail has been released.

9.   Brush the mane with the body brush, making sure you brush underneath the mane, and then run a mane comb through it to 'lay' or 'set' it. Do not use water as this can lead to scurf and irritation from flies in the summer.

Eyes, Nose and Dock

10.   Using clean, tepid water, sponge your horse's eyes and nose. Then take another sponge and clean the dock area. Do not use any kind of soap or shampoo, and make sure you keep each sponge separate for future use. Using different coloured sponges will help to prevent any confusion.

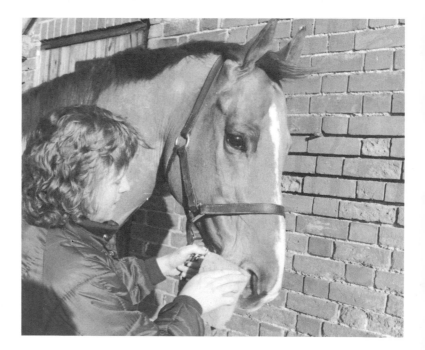

Use clean, tepid water and a clean sponge to wipe your horse's eyes and nose.

11.   To finish off, run over your horse with a clean stable rubber to polish off any excess dust and to bring out the shine.

Finish off by running over your horse with a clean stable rubber to bring out the shine and to remove any excess dust that has re-settled.

GROOMING MACHINES

There are various types of grooming machine: some have revolving heads, others act like a hoover, sucking up the dust from the coat. Those with revolving heads are preferable as they really do get deep into the coat and help to massage the muscles. However, they must be used with caution around manes and tails. While using one, the tail should be bandaged all the way down, and the mane put into long plaits so that neither becomes tangled in the machine. Should this happen the horse may panic, and may never let you near him again with either the grooming machine or the clippers, which can be very frustrating. So in this case prevention is definitely better than cure. As an additional safety measure you should use a circuit breaker, too, so that if the cable is trodden on the machine will automatically turn off. As when grooming normally, you should work

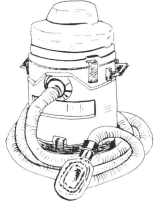

The 'hoover' type of grooming machine which is good for removing scurf and dust.

from the front of the coat backwards, so that all dust and dirt is continually being brushed off. It is a good idea to wear overalls for this job as it can become very messy.

If your horse has never experienced a grooming machine before, introduce it very gradually, as you would clippers. First let him get used to the noise, and only when he appears to be happy should you touch the machine against him. Start at the shoulder and then work around the body until he takes no notice of it wherever you use it. Used regularly, these machines can provide a very valuable daily strapping; the benefits are easily recognized in a horse as its muscles will be well toned up and its coat healthy and shining. They are certainly a boon for the busy horse-owner in this respect, their one drawback being that they can be expensive to buy.

Grooming machines certainly help to promote a healthy, shining coat.

Many traditionalists consider that a horse should always be so well groomed that bathing is unnecessary, but try telling this to the person who has homework to do, or a job to hold down, not to mention a family to look after! We no longer live in times where every horse-owner has his own groom, so such ideals are not practical any more. Owning a horse today means doing the best you can with the time you have, and if this means bathing him every now and again, so be it. There is no evidence to suggest that bathing is detrimental to the horse, providing of course it is carried out at an appropriate time, and that all precautions are taken against him catching a chill afterwards.

Bathing a horse can be good fun for all and very refreshing for him, especially when temperatures are soaring into the eighties. Within reason a horse can be bathed at any time when the weather is warm, although a windy day is not ideal as he will soon begin to feel cold if wet while in a breeze.

Bathing has many benefits: first, it can help to rid the horse of any unwanted coat still unshed; second, using medical shampoos it can help eradicate any parasites or skin complaints; third, it provides a form of massage which stimulates the circulation; and last, it makes the horse feel and look good, which gives you a feeling of satisfaction. At times it is the only really efficient way of removing dulling grease and dust from the coat, so if you have any doubts about bathing your horse, you can forget them and proceed with a clear conscience.

STEP-BY-STEP BATHING TECHNIQUES

1. First of all make sure you have all the items you will require ready to hand: a bucket, horse shampoo, a hose properly connected to a water supply, and a washing mitten or water brush. Then make sure your horse is held in a safe area with no implements that he can hurt himself on if he fidgets. It is safer to have someone hold your horse rather than tie him up, because few horses will stand absolutely still for bathing.

The Body

2. If your horse is happy about you using a hosepipe, then there is no reason why you should not do so. Cold water does not harm the horse, as long as the weather temperature is hot and he has not just

---

DO'S AND DON'TS FOR BATHING A HORSE

- *Do* bath him only on a warm day or during a warm period, especially if he lives out, as this will enable his natural oils to re-establish themselves before a cold spell.
- *Do* have patience. If you start to get annoyed if your horse won't stand still, you will only make matters worse.
- *Don't* use washing-up liquid: buy a properly formulated horse shampoo as these are designed to prevent skin irritations.
- *Don't* put a cold hosepipe on your horse if he has just returned sweating from a tiring ride.
- *Don't* bath your horse within twenty-four hours of a show as his coat will look a little woolly during this period.

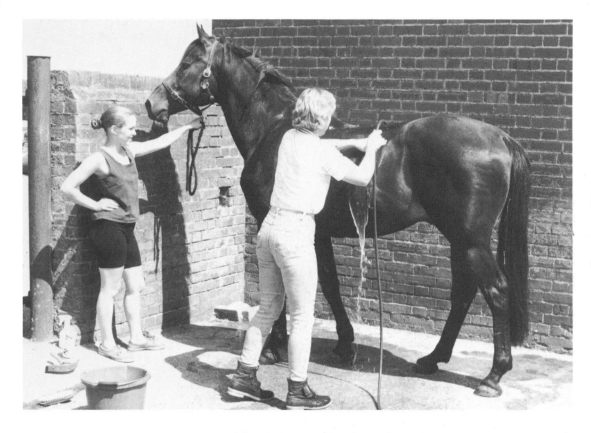

Make sure you only bath your horse on a pleasant, warm day, in an area that is free from implements on which he can hurt himself.

returned from a tiring ride. If your horse is not happy about the use of a hosepipe then you will have to use a bucket and sponge. This can be tiresome and less effective when it comes to rinsing, so spend some time getting your horse used to being hosed over a period of weeks. Start by running the hosepipe over his hoof, then gradually run it up his leg and over his shoulder and neck.

3. Make sure you soak him thoroughly all over one side of his body.

4. Apply the shampoo while he is still fairly wet. Some shampoos need to be diluted: rather than putting the shampoo into a bucket of water, mix it in a clean spray bottle as this makes it easier to apply. Spray it on, then rub it well into the coat using your fingertips in a circular motion, or a washing mitten if you have one. If the coat has dried a little you may have to apply more water to establish a good lather.

5. Be sure to rinse off thoroughly otherwise the shampoo may irri-

Rub the shampoo in well so it makes a good lather.

tate your horse, and he will start rubbing himself. Then repeat the process for the other side of the body.

The Mane

6.   Next, wet the mane thoroughly; if it is too dry it will be very difficult to produce a good lather. Work the shampoo right into the base of the hairs, and rub the hair together until it is completely covered in suds. Pull the forelock back behind the ears so that you can wash it at the same time as the mane.

7.   Again, rinse thoroughly. Flick the mane over to the opposite side to ensure you flush any shampoo out of the base of the mane, and then flick it back, letting the water run freely through the hairs up and down the length of the mane for a couple of minutes.

Wet the mane thoroughly, getting right into the roots.

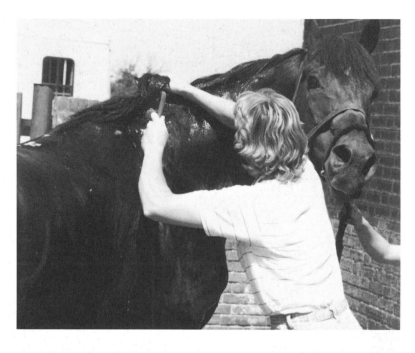

Work the shampoo right into the base of the hairs, until the mane is completely covered in suds.

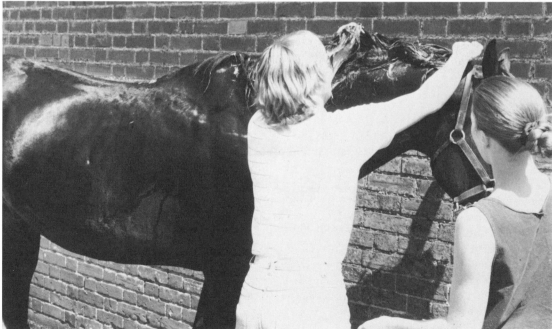

The Tail

8.   If your horse objects to the hosepipe you will have to wash his tail in a bucket of water. Place the whole tail in the bucket, but be prepared for your horse to crouch down on his hindquarters when the water touches the dock. Once thoroughly wet, pull all the hairs apart and work the shampoo right in. Be careful to stand at the side, even if you think your horse will not kick out. Cold water in ticklish places can have unexpected results!

9.   Pay particular attention to the dock area and base of the tail when rinsing, as any shampoo residue can have an effect similar to sweet itch. Once rinsed, squeeze out as much water from the tail as possible, and then swish it round in a circular motion to spin out any remaining water. After washing, put on a tail bandage to encourage the top hairs to lie smooth and flat.

Rinse thoroughly, letting the water run freely through the hairs for a few minutes.

If your horse objects to a hosepipe you will have to dunk the tail into a bucket of water.

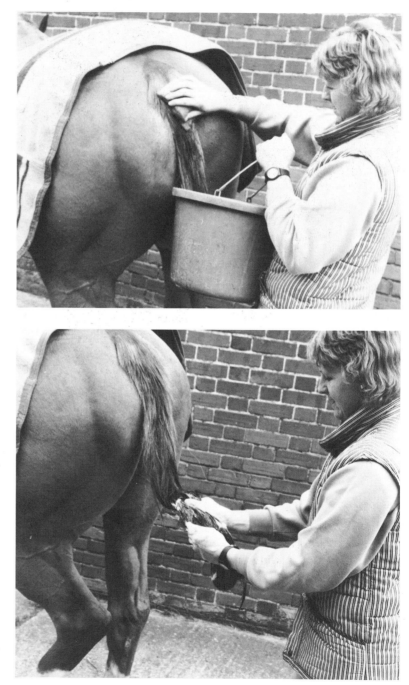

Rub the tail hairs together until a good lather is achieved, then rinse in the bucket, changing the water as many times as is necessary.

Pay particular attention to the dock area and the base of the tail when rinsing.

After washing the tail you can remove much of the excess water by whirling it round for a few seconds.

The Legs

10. These are best washed with a large sponge or a water brush. You may be surprised to see how white socks come up, when previously they were a dirty shade of grey! Be sure to rinse them thoroughly, and then to dry the heels with an old towel or piece of gauze and cotton tissue to avoid the possibility of cracked heels.

The Head

11. With patience, most horses learn to accept their heads being washed, and some like it so much that they try to drink out of the

With patience many horses learn to accept their head being washed, even with a hosepipe.

hosepipe! Make sure that you don't spray the water into your horse's ears or eyes as this can cause problems, and is bound to make him less than co-operative next time.

12.   If your horse will not allow a hosepipe near his head, use a sponge, but be careful that he does not throw his head up and hit you in the face.

13.   If you feel your horse's head requires shampoo, use a very mild one such as a human baby shampoo as this will not sting should it accidentally get into the eyes. Rinse thoroughly, using restraint if necessary, such as the lead rope around his muzzle.

14.   Rinse your horse over again once more and then use a sweat scraper to remove excess water; you will often be surprised to see that you are still scraping out shampoo, even though he looked perfectly rinsed. If this happens, rinse him off again until the sweat scraper reveals no signs of shampoo.

15.   Finally walk your horse round to dry him off. Don't turn him out wet as this will attract the sun which may scald him, and don't leave him wet in his stable as this may result in him getting a chill.

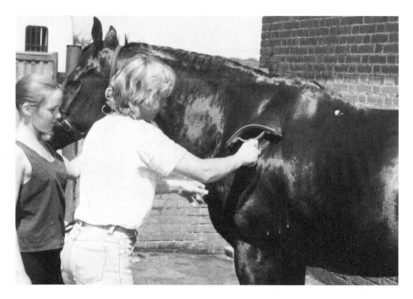

Always use a sweat scraper to remove excess water.

Once your horse is dry, you might like to apply a coat gloss, which will repel dust and dirt. Spraying it onto the mane and tail will also help to keep these tangle free, thus saving labour when it comes to grooming, and also ensuring a nice thick tail as continual brushing can thin the hairs. Once the horse has had a chance to rest, it is a good idea to give him a thorough grooming with a clean body brush, as this will help to restore the natural coat oils as quickly as possible.

CHILL PREVENTION

Having bathed your horse you need to protect him against catching a chill while drying, even in warm weather. If there is no breeze and it is very hot, walking him around the yard should be sufficient to dry him off while keeping him warm. If it is a little windy, or the sun goes behind a cloud, it is a sensible precaution to rug or 'thatch' your horse. Rugging a wet horse can be tricky, as it is important that the water is allowed to evaporate. The best way of doing this is to put on a sweat rug (the string vest type) with a summer sheet on top; this will provide a layer of air next to the skin which will keep the body warm while it dries. Thatching employs the same principle: to thatch a horse, first cover him in a layer of straw, then put the summer sheet on over the top of this and secure it with a surcingle or roller. Once

A light summer sheet or cooler put on over the top of a traditional sweat rug will provide an insulating layer of warm air next to the skin, which prevents a horse from catching a chill while drying after a bath.

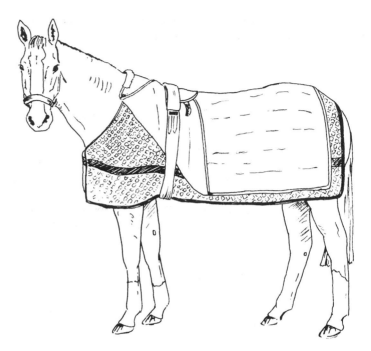

Thatching is another method of preventing the horse from catching a chill when wet: a layer of clean, soft straw is arranged over the horse's back and quarters, and a summer sheet put on top of this to secure it and to prevent the warm air from escaping too quickly.

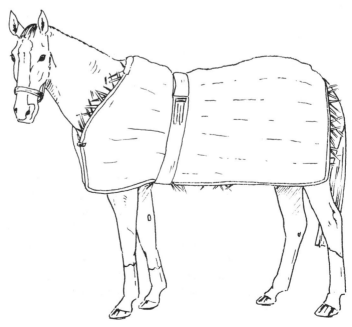

dry, rub your horse over with a clean stable rubber, and then he may be turned out or put back into his stable as normal.

STAIN REMOVAL

Sometimes you may not wish to give your horse a full bath, but need to remove a stubborn stain that won't brush out. This is a particular problem for owners of grey horses, as these stains always look unsightly. To remove stable stains, dampen the hair with tepid water (this can be done in winter or summer); apply a little mild shampoo, or hypo-allergenic soap, rubbing it well in with the fingertips or water brush until the stain is removed. Rinse thoroughly with a sponge and tepid water, and then dry completely with an old towel.

WASHING THE GENITALS

This procedure needs to be carried out more regularly than a complete bath, so it is a good idea to take care of it at the weekly complete groom. A gelding will need his sheath washed, and a mare her vulva and udder. Use warm water and a mild soap and be sure to rinse thoroughly. At first your horse may object, especially if this part of his hygiene has been overlooked by a previous owner, which is regrettably quite common; if this is the case, have someone hold up a front leg to prevent the horse from fidgeting. On no account should you use a cold hosepipe, and always dry these areas once clean. An in-season mare may need her genitals cleaned every day, but be more careful at this time as she may be more temperamental.

SPONGING AFTER WORK

It is acceptable to wash a sweaty horse down after work although he should not be given a full bath. He will find it refreshing, rather like us having a shower after, say, a hard game of squash. However, you should be as efficient as possible. The horse will derive most benefit if you sponge off the areas where the tack has been, and under the elbows and between the hind legs. Obviously there is no need to shampoo him, but you will need to use the sweat scraper to remove as much water as you can, and rug him up afterwards as previously described, to prevent chilling.

Trimming is carried out for purely cosmetic reasons in order to make the horse look smart; when done correctly it can make a huge difference to the way he looks, which may be crucial in the show ring. However, a horse which lives out will need some protection from mud on his legs and flies around his face, so consider how you keep your horse before giving him a haircut; or at least offer extra protection if you do take away his natural defences. The horse which is in regular work will just need a little trim up from time to time, whereas the horse which has been turned away for the winter and left to grow his hair normally, is likely to require quite a lot of attention and trimming, to the head, ears, legs, heels, coronet and bridle patch. Obviously, how much hair needs to be removed will depend on the type or breed of horse; a cob or a native pony will have far more hair than a Thoroughbred or an Arab, for instance.

STEP-BY-STEP TRIMMING TECHNIQUES

The Head

1. You can start to trim anywhere you like, but it is often a good idea to trim the head first, before the horse starts to get fed up and fidgety. Long hair around the face is unsightly and can get caught up in the bridle, so it is best removed if the horse is in work. Such hairs also tend to make the head look bulky, when in the show ring what you are aiming for is a smart, streamlined appearance.
2. If your horse accepts clippers on his face then you can use these to get the job done quickly and neatly. If not, to ensure an even finish you should use a mane comb and scissors. Use the type of scissors that are slightly curved; these can be obtained from most good saddlers and are excellent for trimming whiskers as they angle away from the skin and so the horse cannot be accidentally nicked. First, remove any long hairs with the scissors alone, but do not cut too close to the face. Then push the mane comb up through the hair against the lie of the coat so that it stands up, and cut straight against the edge of the mane comb.
3. Removing thick or long hair from under the jaw will make the head look more streamlined. If the side of the face has 'cat hairs', remove these carefully, being sure not to clip the short hair underneath. A good way to prevent this is to hold the knuckles of your hand against the jaw as you clip.
4. A stabled horse can have all his whiskers removed, but a horse

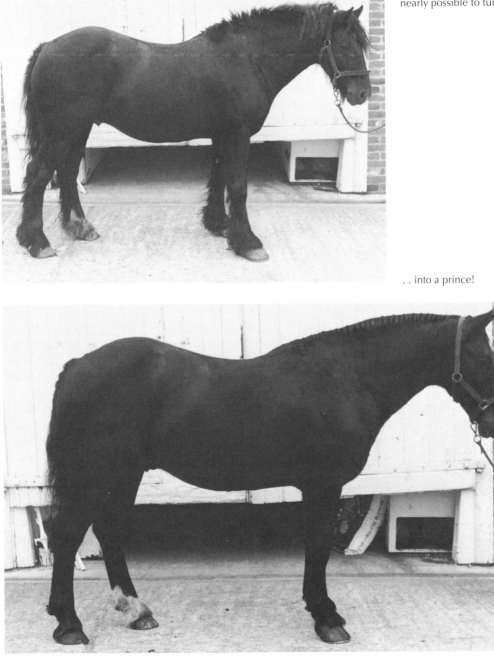

With a little bit of trimming it is nearly possible to turn a frog . . .

. . into a prince!

(a) Coarse 'cat hairs' and long facial hair can be removed in order to give the horse a more streamlined look.

(b) Start by simply cutting the long hairs with a pair of scissors, but be careful not to go too near the face.

(c) Push a mane comb against the lie of the hairs so that they stand up, then cut against the edge of the mane comb. This ensures a natural, rather than a 'freshly cut' look.

(d) Once completed, the horse's features will look far more refined.

a

b

c

d

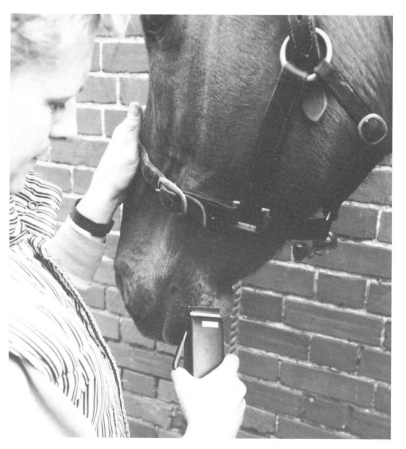

A stabled horse can have all his whiskers removed, but a horse at grass should have some left in place for protection.

at grass should have some left in place for protection. If the horse is ridden in a noseband with a lower chin strap, or wears a curb chain, it is a good idea to clip off the whiskers around the curb groove to prevent them getting caught in the tack and pinching him.

The Ears

5.   The ears can also be trimmed: squeeze both edges of the ear together and run the clippers (or scissors) along the outside edge.
6.   Then let the ear open as normal and just trim up any long or bushy bits that have escaped. Do not remove all the hair from inside the ear, because it acts as a filter against dust, flies and other foreign objects. The result should be a sharp outline to the ears, rather than a fuzzy look.

(a) The long hairs which stick out of the ears can be removed to improve the horse's appearance.

(b) Pinch the two sides of the ear together and cut along the outside edge.

(c) Let the ear open as normal, and tidy up any remaining long or bushy hairs.

(d) The finished result, a nice neat outline which will enhance the horse's head.

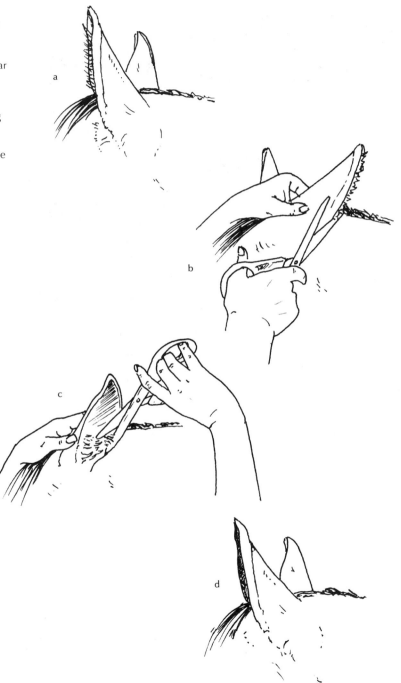

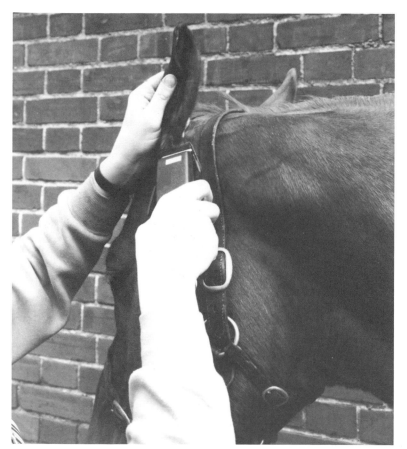

Hand-held battery clippers are excellent for trimming up the ears as they are practically silent.

The Legs

7. Excessive hair on the lower legs can be trimmed away, but remember that feathers do offer protection against mud fever so don't trim them if your horse lives out in a muddy field. When trimming the legs do not kneel down, because if the horse moves suddenly you will not be able to jump up and out of the way in time.
8. Again, you can use clippers, but if your horse dislikes them then use a mane comb and scissors. How you trim the legs will depend upon the type of horse you have: for the fine-boned horse, run the clippers down the leg with the lie of the coat; for the more thick-set horse that has coarse hair and full feathers, run the clippers up against the lie of the hair to give a sharp outline. If using a mane

(a) If using a mane comb and scissors, push the mane comb under the hair and lift it away from the leg; then snip along the comb.

(b) If the hair around the coronets is also very long, use the same technique to thin it out first.

(c) Then snip around the edge to ensure a neat line.

(d) A neat and tidy finish, which often makes a horse look far less common.

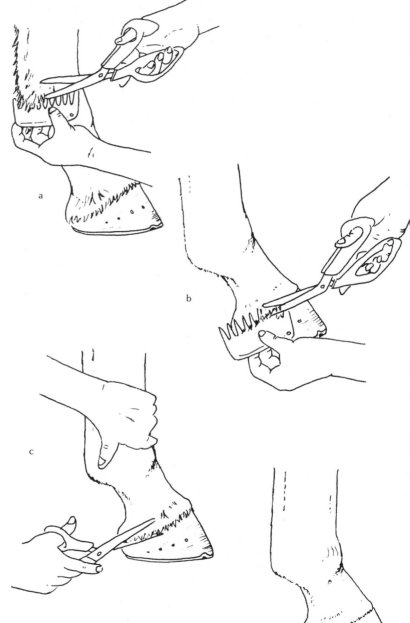

a

b

c

d

comb and scissors, push the mane comb under the hair and lift it away from the leg; then snip along the comb. This prevents the horse from finishing up with a leg that looks as though rats have gnawed it.

9.   If your horse's ergots protrude a great deal you will need to trim these down, too; a pair of secateurs or farrier's pincers are ideal for this job. Be careful not to trim them too close to the skin, or they will be sore; the truly 'dead' section will be hard and flaky. Often if you first give the ergot a little pull, it will start to come away at an appropriate place of its own accord; then simply snip it off.

Heels

10.   Few horses have a lot of hair on their heels, except those with a high proportion of draught or native blood. A horse that lives out does need the protection offered by this hair, so do not trim it off; for the stabled horse, however, you can trim a certain amount. This should always be done with scissors, as the clippers cannot get in properly and may 'nick' the bulbs of the heel. Do not attempt to follow the contours of the heel, but just trim straight across so that it looks neat and tidy.

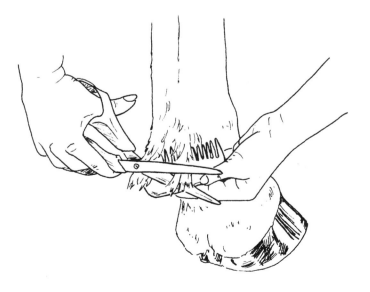

Whether or not you trim the feathers depends upon whether your horse lives out or in a stable. If you do trim them, use the same technique as for the rest of the leg.

SINGEING

As its name implies, this is a process whereby the horse's hair is singed rather than cut; before the advent of electric clippers, singeing was very common. It is still practised today, however, as it leaves a smooth, natural finish rather than that 'newly trimmed' look. Singeing is only used to burn off the coarse 'cat hairs' that appear on the clipped horse's beard and around the throat in the spring time. To singe these hairs you need either a proper singeing lamp (*see* illustration), or a candle. Great care must be taken to avoid burning the horse's coat or skin. Hold the lamp away from the face, gradually bringing it nearer until the hairs shrivel up and disappear. Do not expect your horse to accept this process straightaway: it may take a few sessions before he comes to realize that it is not frightening, and only then is he likely to stand patiently and allow you to do as you wish.

Coronets

11.   Trim round the coronets to finish off. On the whole this is done with scissors or it will look ragged, although bushy, coarse hair can be trimmed with the clippers against the lie of the coat. If using clippers, always make sure you do the job at least a week before a show as this gives the hair time to lie flat again, rather than standing up on end.

Bridle Patch

12.   Making a bridle patch involves trimming away about a 1in (2.5cm) section of mane from behind the ears; this enables the bridle or headcollar headpiece to sit flat and secure over the poll. Clippers will be too wide for this job, so use the scissors. Use a mane comb to make a neat parting between the forelock and the section to be trimmed, then clip off the selected area right down close to the skin. If your horse has a very sparse forelock and you plait him a lot, you might not want to trim this area at all, as it will remove valuable hair for plaiting.

Withers

13.   You can also trim a short 2 to 3in (5 to 7.5cm) section of mane away from the withers if this causes trouble by getting tangled up under the rugs, saddle or numnah. This area rarely has enough hair to make a plait, and even if it did, it would not enhance the neckline, so it does look tidier if it is trimmed.

A singeing lamp. These can be very hard to acquire, so you can improvise by the careful use of a candle.

HOGGING A MANE

A hogged mane is one that has been completely removed, forelock as well. Generally only cobs and polo ponies are hogged, although some riding schools also hog the manes of native types with thick, bushy hair to prevent it getting tangled up in the reins. Occasionally a mane may need to be hogged for veterinary purposes, perhaps to facilitate the treatment of sweet itch or lice, for example. However, hogging is quite a drastic step as it removes one of the horse's main defences against flies, so you should ask yourself whether it is really necessary before doing it.

Hogging is certainly a job for the clippers; scissors would leave an untidy finish and would be very hard going. Before starting, give the mane a good brush through to remove as much scurf from the roots as possible; dirt and scurf will clog up and blunt the clipper blades. Make sure your horse is quite happy about the clippers; give him a few minutes to become accustomed to them if necessary. When hogging the mane, clip right down to the root of the hair, but be sure not to clip into the horse's coat on either side of the crest, or to nick the skin. Put your hand over the horse's eye when clipping the forelock to ensure no hair falls in.

In his natural state the horse needs his mane as protection against flies, so if you remove this protection you must offer him an alternative. You might consider putting on a fly fringe and using an effective fly repellent, or you could use a light linen hood and neck cover if your horse does not object. Hogged manes do tend to become scurfy if not bathed regularly. To help combat this problem, rub the top of the neck daily with a mixture of witch hazel and garlic; not only does this help to combat the build-up of dirt and scurf, it helps to keep flies away.

While with plaiting you can enhance a horse's appearance by strategically placing the plaits, when hogging a mane there is no disguising your horse's neck: once the mane has gone, your horse's neckline is on show for all to see. If you are hogging your horse's mane to show him in a cob class, think about this before going ahead, and perhaps take steps to build up a correct top line first.

Once a mane has been hogged, it will require regular trimming every month, although some horses' manes may grow at a quicker or slower rate than this. Should you wish to let a hogged mane grow out, it can take between one and two years to establish itself again, and may need to be trained over by leaving it in long plaits for a time – another reason to think carefully before deciding to hog.

The purpose of pulling a horse's mane is to flatter his image and make the job of plaiting easier. A neatly pulled mane can often change the appearance of a horse's neck almost completely, which may be especially useful if it is not his strongest conformation point. A pulled mane can also be of benefit to those who tend to get their horse's mane tangled up in the reins; and of course it makes grooming easier. However, there are certain breeds which, for show purposes, should not have their manes or tails pulled, so check with your breed society if you are in any doubt about your horse and you want to show him.

It is easier if you pull your horse's mane or tail after work or in warm weather as his pores will be open and so the hair will pull out far more easily. Most manes are pulled to between 4in (10cm) and 6in (15cm), although you should take into account the type of mane when deciding the ideal length. Thus a finer mane will need to be left longer, in order that plaits of a decent size can still be made; whereas a bushy mane will need to be thinned considerably but if it is pulled too short, it will start to stick up, rather than lie over.

HUMANE ALTERNATIVES

Pulling the mane and tail is an uncomfortable process for the horse and, in the majority of cases, other methods can be substituted and used to extremely good effect. Careful razoring with a thinning comb or single clipper blade is a kind, efficient alternative, and with practice can also save time.

A mane in need of pulling if it is to be neatly plaited.

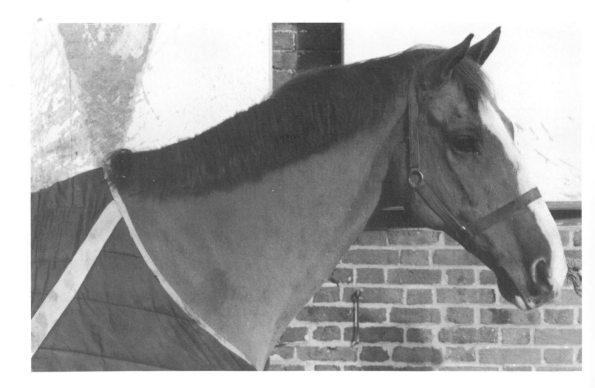

STEP-BY-STEP MANE PULLING TECHNIQUES

1.   First, brush the mane through with a mane comb so that it lies flat. You can start from the base of the mane, or near your horse's ears, whichever he objects to the least. From underneath his mane, take hold of a few strands in one hand. With a short mane comb, push the remaining hairs upwards towards his neckline.
2.   Next, pull quickly and firmly on the strands in your hand.
3.   If the hair does not come out easily then you may have to wrap it round the mane comb to provide some leverage. However, make sure you are not trying to pull out too much at once, and continually check your horse's crest to ensure it is not bleeding. If you do see spots of blood, stop pulling immediately and wait at least a day before continuing. If you keep on pulling until you reach a point where the horse is sore, not only is it unacceptable to treat him in such a manner, but he may also start to rub the mane in order to try to relieve his discomfort. This can often lead to the extreme of the horse rubbing his mane so badly that he has little left to pull, and what he does have left you will certainly be unable to plait, so be warned!

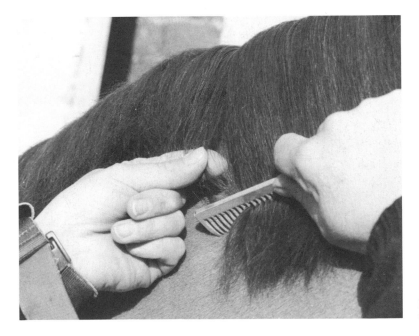

Brush the mane through with a mane comb so that it lies flat.

Take hold of a few strands from underneath the mane and push the remaining hair back towards the neckline.

If the hair does not come out easily you may have to wrap it round the mane comb.

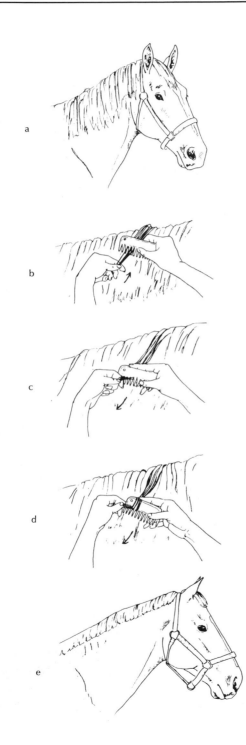

(a) A long mane in need of pulling if it is to be plaited.
(b) Start by taking hold of a few strands of hair and running the mane comb up towards the neck line.
(c) Pull the strands out a few at a time.
(d) If the hair does not come out easily, you may need to wrap it round the comb to provide a little leverage.
(e) The desired result is an even mane of between 4in (10cm), and 6in (15cm) long.

How not to pull a mane: it should be shortened evenly along its entire length, not a section at a time.

4.   Work along in very small sections at a time, aiming to shorten and thin the mane as you go. Do not pull the top hairs of the mane, because when they regrow they will stick up like the bristles of a brush.

5.   Do not be in too much of a hurry: it may take a few sessions over a period of days before the mane is short and neat. If your horse looks a little untidy for a few days while you are in the process of pulling the mane, then it is just too bad.

6.   You may have to work along the mane from top to bottom two or three times before you get it to the length you want. Do not set out to pull a whole section at a time, so that you end up with one section the required length with the rest of the mane still long (*see* illustration), but shorten it evenly all the way along. Brush the mane after each go at it, to ensure you are working in a straight line. Then you can fiddle about plucking out the odd strand here and there until

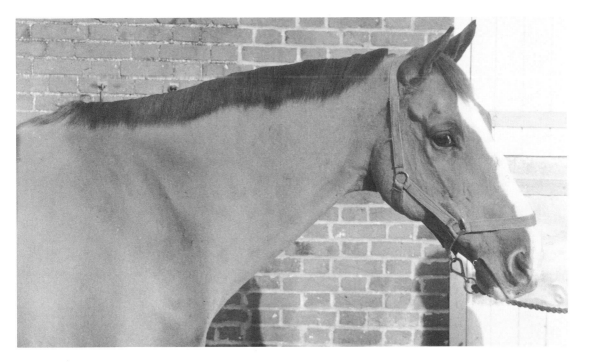

you get it looking nice and neat. Don't worry if your first attempt is a little crooked; it does take practice, but as long as you go slowly your horse shouldn't object.

7. Pull the forelock in the same manner. Most forelocks do not need as much thinning as the mane, so be cautious, or you will end up with nothing to plait.

Should your horse have been treated roughly in the past he may already object to having his mane pulled, in which case you will have to be very gentle and only pull a few strands each day. If he will not tolerate it at all, you may have to twitch him, or to concede that out of kindness it may be best to use a thinning comb which razors the hair to the correct length. Alternatively you can use a clipper blade which does the same job: you pull the hairs taut and razor them off a section at a time. Sometimes this 'razoring' technique is preferable even when a horse is quite amenable to having his mane pulled: where a horse has a very thin, wispy mane anyway, pulling would simply exacerbate the problem and in such a case razoring will shorten, but not thin the mane, so it can still be effectively plaited.

Don't worry if your first attempt is a little crooked; pulling a mane does take practice.

In no circumstances should you simply cut the mane with a pair of scissors. This looks awful and makes the ends very bristly, which makes the task of plaiting far more difficult.

Most professionals always pull the tails of mainstream show horses such as hunters, riding horses and cobs, rather than plaiting them: first, because it shows off the hindquarters better; second, because it is more convenient – it obviates the need for time-consuming plaiting – and third, because they feel that constant plaiting weakens the top of the tail.

When done correctly, a pulled tail can really show off a horse's hindquarters. However, it is more difficult to pull a tail properly than it is a mane, and some people never manage to master the art. It would appear that this is largely because they have neither the experience nor the patience; but if you are prepared to acquire these vital qualities, there is no reason why you should not become proficient at it. Admittedly some tails are easier to pull than others – it is very hard to make a coarse-haired, fat dock look elegant, for instance – but nonetheless the appearance of *all* tails can be improved by neat pulling.

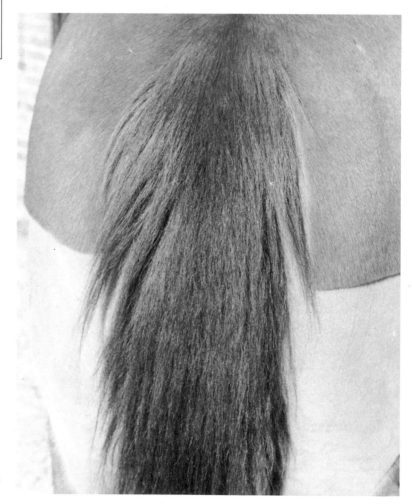

All tails can be improved by neat pulling.

Again, consideration needs to be given to the way the horse is kept. A horse living out in the summer will need the protection of a full, natural tail to ward off flies and other irritating midges. Similarly in the winter a naturally growing tail helps to provide protection from the wind and rain. In addition you should check the rules for your showing category before pulling your horse's tail, in case your breed of horse should be shown with a full tail.

STEP-BY-STEP TAIL PULLING TECHNIQUES

To pull a tail you should work in the same manner as the mane – though be aware that more horses object to their tails being pulled, so be careful and very gentle, working over several days. Inevitably you need to stand to the rear of the horse, so take precautions against being kicked when pulling a tail by operating over the stable door (*see* illustration). As with mane pulling, working the horse first will help the hairs to come out more easily, as he will be warm and thus his pores will be open.

In the interests of safety, always pull your horse's tail over the top of a stable door.

1. Firstly brush out the tail, removing all the scurf you can.
2. Start by pulling a few underneath strands from the top on either side of the tail.
3. As with the mane, you may need to wrap the strands round a mane comb in order to remove them; this will also help to prevent your fingers from becoming sore.
4. Be careful not to pull the hairs on the front centre of the tail too short, otherwise they will start to stick up and look like a hedgehog. Some tails are quite fine, and so do not require any pulling of these front hairs.

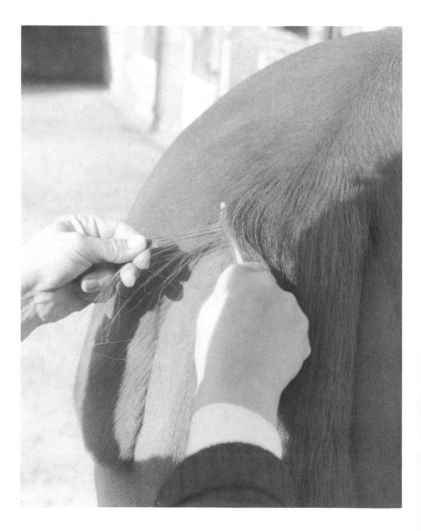

Start by pulling a few underneath hairs from the top on either side of the tail.

You may need to wrap the hair round the comb if it does not come out easily.

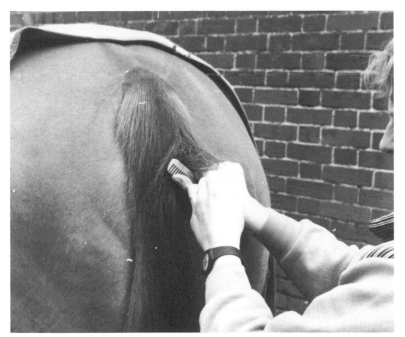

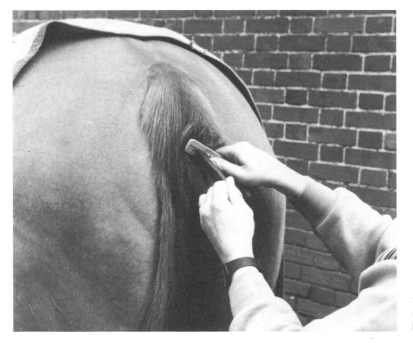

The hairs on the front of the tail may not need much pulling, so be careful not to over-do it.

How a pulled tail should look once finished.

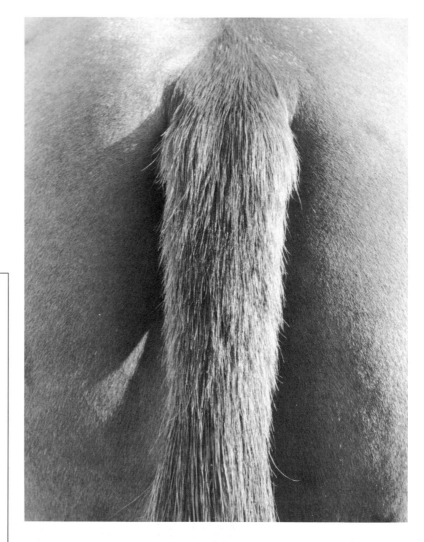

HUMANE ALTERNATIVES

Unlike the mane, the tail will rarely interfere with tack, so unless you need to plait a very thick or bushy tail it is questionable whether thinning is necessary at all. If it is, the kind alternative to pulling is to tidy the tail with a clipper blade or a thinning comb, although it is undoubtedly more difficult to achieve a satisfactory result than it is when this method is used on the mane. However, for the sake of the horse's comfort it is well worth experimenting with it: with practice it is possible to improve the tail's appearance without subjecting the horse to the discomfort that pulling entails.

5. How far down the dock you go depends on the shape and condition of your horse's hindquarters. As a rough guide, most people pull about half the length of their horse's dock, which usually coincides with the widest point of its hindquarters; this is often somewhere between 7 and 8in (18 and 20cm) in length.

6. Once the tail has been pulled, put on a tail bandage for an hour or so each day to encourage the hair to lie and grow flat. This will facilitate pulling next time round, and will help the tail to keep a neat shape at the top, rather than growing out in an unruly fashion.

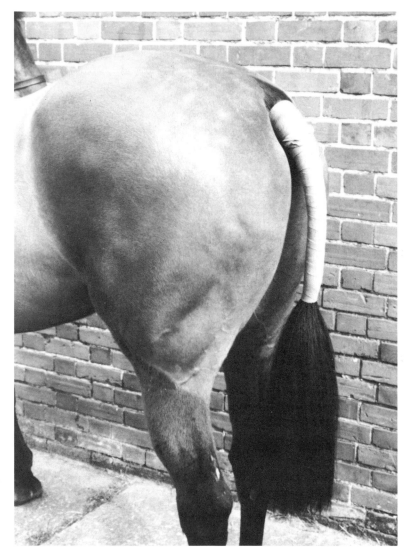

Putting on a tail bandage regularly will encourage the tail to lie flat, and grow flat, too.

BANGING THE TAIL

Having pulled the top of the tail, it is important to ensure the rest of it also looks smart. Ask someone to put an arm under your horse's dock, and then trim off the bottom of his tail into a straight line; this is known as a banged tail, and makes for a very smart finish. You can

(a) A naturally growing tail; (b) a pulled tail; (c) a bandaged and banged tail

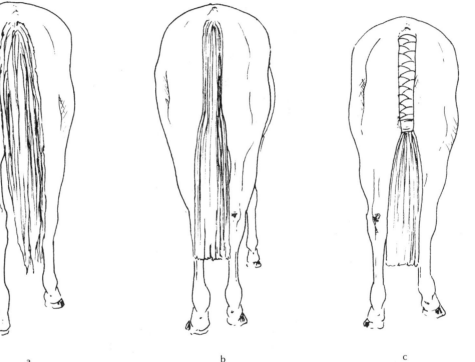

a   b   c

SWITCH TAIL

A switch tail describes a tail where the pulling of the top continues until half its length has been pulled, or in some cases all of it. The ends are then left to form a natural point at the bottom. This practice is now far less popular than it used to be, and may well die out over the next few years.

use scissors for this job, but if your horse has a bushy tail, you may end up with a rather ragged line so use a clipper blade instead to slice through the hair at the correct length: for a tail this is about 2 to 4in (5 to 10cm) below the hocks. However, before trimming it to this length you need to take note of the horse's natural tail carriage: if he carries it high, you will need to leave it a little longer, or vice versa. Having judged the ideal length for each individual horse, have someone put his arm underneath the dock to hold the tail at the height and angle that mirrors the horse's natural carriage; then trim it straight as it falls while in this position.

It is a good idea to wash and brush the tail before banging it to free any tangles, so making sure that each strand is cut to the right length. It also ensures you do not get blisters on your fingers from trying to cut through mud and grease as well as the hairs!

Have someone hold the tail in a way that reflects your horse's natural tail carriage before you straighten it at the bottom.

Take note of your horse's natural tail carriage before banging the tail.

While the purpose of a plaited mane is to show off the horse's neck in order to make him look much more elegant in the ring, it is also a practical way of keeping the mane out of the way of the reins. While riding in the show ring, plaits will be put up in the normal way, but there is no reason why you should not put long plaits in a thick, unpulled mane for everyday riding if this helps to keep the reins under control. Plaiting in this way can also help to train an unruly mane to lie over to one side, usually the off (right)-side of the horse.

If a mane has been well pulled it will be easier to plait in the normal way, although there are other plaiting techniques that can be used for longer manes (see sections on Running Plait, Spanish Plait, later in this chapter). Always remember that it is far more difficult to plait a newly washed mane, so if for any reason you need to wash the mane, do so at least a whole day before a show, if not two or three days beforehand. If it is essential that the mane is kept scrupulously clean in between washing and the show day, you can use a linen hood, or a more protective one if your horse is turned out.

When plaiting a mane, use a needle and thread rather than elastic bands, as these do not secure the plaits so well, and can damage the mane if used regularly. If plaiting for the show ring, plaits should be secured with cotton of a colour as similar to the mane as possible; white cotton on black or chestnut manes is fine for dressage, but it is not correct for showing. While it may take up to an hour to plait a mane if it is something new to you, with practice you will soon be plaiting a whole mane within twenty minutes to half an hour.

HOW MANY PLAITS?

It is entirely up to you how many plaits you use. At one time it was traditional to use only seven up the neck with the forelock plait making eight. However, this practice has now died out as people found they needed to use more or fewer plaits according to the length and conformation of the individual horse's neck. The custom of having an odd number of plaits up the neck remains, however, with the forelock plait always making an even number. Nor is this a matter of pot luck, because you should always aim to accentuate your horse's neck by using plaits strategically; this includes both the number of plaits and the size or type of plait you use. For example, you can make a short neck look longer by using more, smaller plaits

a

b

You can improve the appearance of your horse's neck by the strategic placing of plaits the right size and number for your horse: (a) a weak topline can be improved by sitting the plaits up along the crest of the neck; (b) a short, thick-set neck will be improved if the plaits are tucked neatly down to the side.

along the neck; and conversely, fewer large plaits can make a longer neck look shorter. Where you position the plaits will also create a certain effect. Thus a weak topline can be improved by sitting the plaits up along the crest of the neck, whereas a thick-set neck will be improved if the plaits are tucked neatly down to the side. As you can see, plaiting is an art and as you do it more regularly you will begin to acquire an 'eye' for what will suit each horse.

STEP-BY-STEP MANE PLAITING TECHNIQUES

1. First, gather your plaiting kit together and tie the horse where there is a hard flat surface; this will help you to retrieve any needles you may accidentally drop – needles dropped in bedding are a great worry, and bring home the old saying of finding a needle in a haystack! Once ready to start, brush the mane really well to remove any dirt or scurf, and then comb it so that it lies nice and flat.
2. Part the mane into sections and secure them by using plaiting bands. Plastic bulldog hair clips are a great help when plaiting as they hold unwanted sections out of the way until needed. If it is to

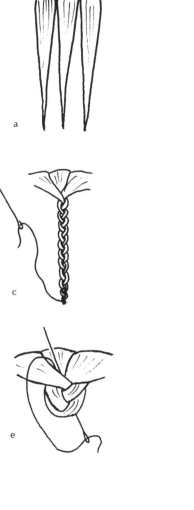

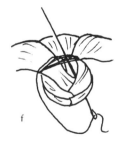

(a) Dividing one section into three; (b) plaiting down; (c) securing the bottom of the plait; (d) folding up; (e) folding up again, to produce a nice, neat finish; (f) securing the whole of the plait by passing the thread around it a few times; (g) cutting off the thread underneath the plait;

(h) the end result should be neat and appealing.

look neat when finished, a thicker mane will need more sections (and so more plaits as a result) than a thinner one. In general, most manes usually accommodate between seven and thirteen plaits, although as already discussed, this is not a rule.

Part the mane into sections ready for plaiting.

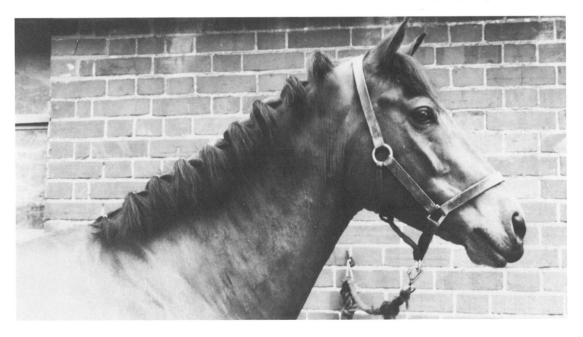

3. Take the first section in your hands, working from poll to withers, or vice-versa if you prefer, and divide it into three. You can buy a neat little gadget which will do this for you if you have trouble in getting three even divisions (*see* illustration).

4. Then plait the hair down, taking the right section over the middle, then the left section over the middle and so on, so that all the strands alternate round. Keep the tension fairly tight as this makes for an even plait when finished.

5. When you can plait no further, sew round the bottom with a needle and thread to prevent the plait from unwinding. Make a small loop, and then sew around this, too, to prevent any stray hairs from poking out of the plait when finished.

6. With the needle and cotton still attached to the plait, push the needle up through the base of the plait in the centre.

7. Pull upwards so that the plait folds under itself, making a loop. Then put the needle back through the bottom of the loop and pull up once more so that the loop doubles up making a 'ball' or 'plait'.

8. Push the needle up through the centre again, and this time take it round to the left and then up through the base of the plait, and then repeat the process to the right. Do this a few times to secure the whole plait.

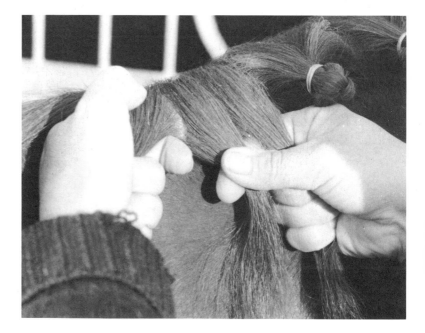

Divide each section into three equal size strands.

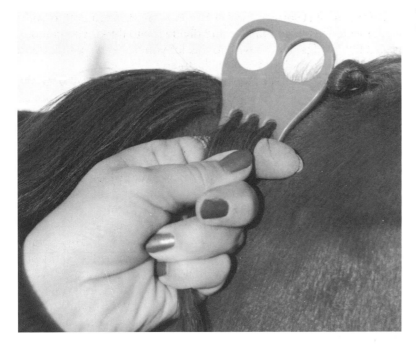

This little gadget will divide the mane equally into three for you if you experience any difficulty.

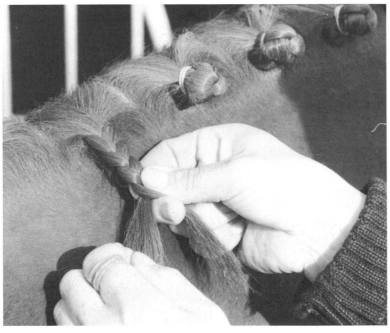

Continue plaiting down, taking the right section over the middle, then the left section over the middle and so on.

When you can plait no further,
secure the end to prevent it from
unwinding.

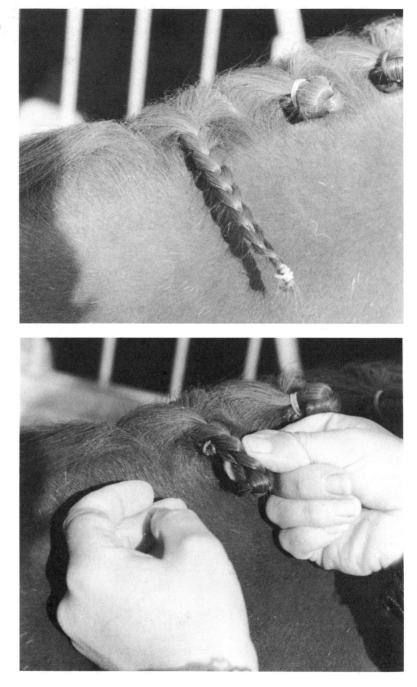

Fold the plait up underneath
itself, until it makes a neat ball.

Proceed down the mane until it is all neatly plaited.

9. Run the cotton round the base of the whole plait and then push the needle down through the plait (*not* into the horse's neck!) and knot it through a section of the underneath hairs. Cut it close to the knot making sure that no ugly lumps or straggling ends of cotton remain visible.

10. Proceed down the mane until all the plaits are secured and even. Remember to secure each plait *underneath*.

11. You can plait the forelock in a similar way; it is often easiest to start off with, although if it is particularly thick you may need to use a French plait (*see* below).

12. When removing plaits, be very careful not to cut any of the mane. An ordinary dressmaker's seam stripper is very useful to have when removing plaits, as it prevents this from happening.

FRENCH PLAITING A FORELOCK

French plaiting a forelock is very similar to plaiting a tail. It is a useful technique if the forelock is either fairly bushy or long, and it makes

A French plaited forelock.

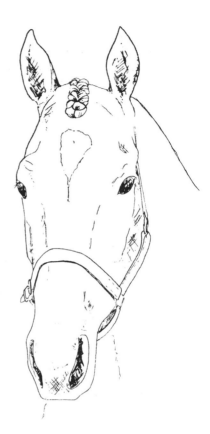

a neat job of what would otherwise be one rather large plait sitting between the horse's ears.

1.   First, comb out any tangles and make sure all the hair strands are separated. This is very important, as otherwise you will not be able to pull small amounts of hair in from the sides.

2.   If you dampen the hair you may find it more manageable, but often this is not necessary.

3.   From the very back of the forelock (the hairs just in front of the bridle patch), take a small section of hair and divide it into two; do not start off with too much hair – as a guide, when flat each section should not be more than about ½in (1cm) across. Cross these two sections over, so that the right-hand one is on the left and vice versa. This makes the start of the plait neat and tidy, preventing it from standing away from the skin.

4.   Take another section of hair the same size from one side, so that you now have three sections.

5.   Start to plait these sections down as normal, crossing the right-hand section over the middle one, and then the left-hand one over the middle. However, as you cross each section over, merge in with another section of an equal quantity of hair from the same side.

6.   When you reach the base of the forelock, there will be no hair left to take in from the side, so simply continue plaiting down the three strands that you have, as normal.

7.   Fasten the end with needle and thread, and put it up in the normal way (*see* Mane Plaiting Techniques, above).

RUNNING PLAIT

Not everyone wants to conform to a traditional standard, and if you are not competing in a class that demands a certain turnout, there is no reason why you should not experiment when plaiting your horse's mane. There are a few other ways of plaiting a mane which although not common, are most useful where the mane needs to be left long, or in its natural state. The running plait is mostly used to tidy up a mane that cannot be pulled, for whatever reason. It is not used in the show ring, but often provides the solution for an owner who needs to leave his pony's mane long for showing, but wants to have it neat and tidy when jumping or undertaking some other activity.

1.   First, brush out the mane and then comb it as if you were going to plait normally.

2.   Single out a section of the mane from just behind the bridle patch, about the same size as for a normal plait.

3.   Begin to plait this down, and as you cross the hair held in your left hand over the middle section, bring in another section of mane with it. (This relates to plaiting a mane lying on the off-side of the neck; simply reverse the instructions if your pony's mane lies on the near-side.)

4.   Continue to take in a section of the mane each time you cross over; you will soon see the mane curve round at the top, and then level off into one long plait lying parallel to the crest.

5.   Do not pull the plait tight, otherwise it will not hang correctly, but just let the hair come in as it falls naturally. Each section you take in should be of equal size if the plait is to be neat.

6.   When you get down to the end of the mane near the withers, continue to plait down with the three strands that you have.

A running plait.

7.   Secure this at the end with needle and thread, then loop any straggling ends around this and again wrap the thread around the whole lot so that no ends are poking out. Sometimes the mane is so bushy that this is very difficult to do. In such cases you can use a little insulating tape of the same colour as the mane, simply wrapping it around the loose hairs at the end of the plait.

8.   The forelock can be finished off with a normal, or French plait, as the size of the mane warrants.

SPANISH PLAIT

This is an extremely elegant plait, used mainly to decorate a long, thick mane that is otherwise left long for showing. It is not a plait that is used for showing, but can be seen in the fancy dress ring, on gymkhana ponies, or those in various parades.

1.   There are two techniques: the single or double Spanish plait, although both are accomplished in the same way. A single plait is used for a finer mane on only one side of the neck, while a double plait is used for a longer, thicker mane on both sides of the neck.

2.   To do a double plait, divide the mane equally down the centre of the horse's neck so that half lies on the off-side and half on the near-side.

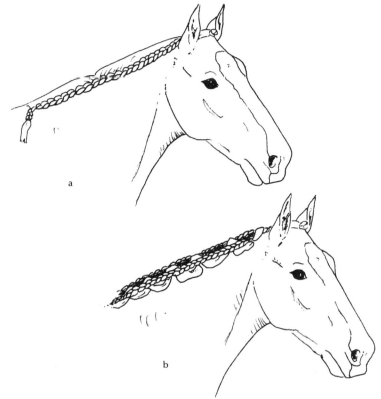

(a) A single Spanish plait, and (b) a double Spanish plait, which has been decorated with ribbons.

a

b

3.   Take up one side of the mane, and single out one section to start plaiting with as normal. The idea of this plait is that you keep it as close to the crest as possible, and do not let it hang down one side of the neck as with the running plait. You should therefore take sections in from the mane, as with the running plait, but keep it tight into the crest. If you could imagine sitting on the horse's back and plaiting from the poll, down towards yourself, this will give you the idea.

4.   Once you come to the end, plait down the three strands as normal and if doing a double plait secure temporarily with a plaiting band; if not, secure permanently with needle and thread and finish as for the running plait.

5.   Repeat the process on the other side of the neck, if doing a double plait.

6.   Having finished both sides you will be left with the two plait ends. Remove the plaiting bands and merge the hair together, being

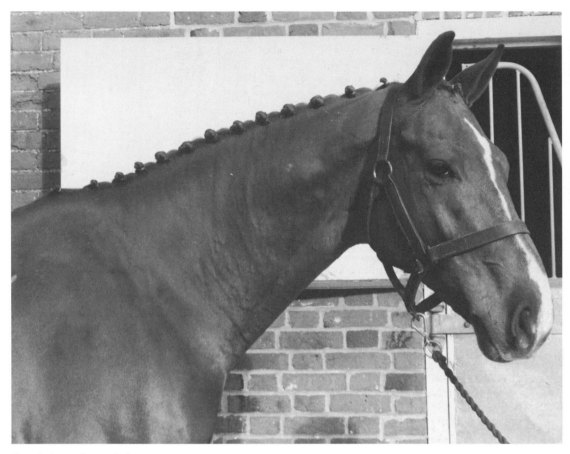

Short hairs can be stuck down with gel until they grow long enough to be incorporated into the plaits.

careful not to allow the rest of the mane to unravel. Divide this merged hair into three sections and plait these down. Fasten as normal.

7. If taking part in a parade, you can also plait ribbons in as you go, or weave them through from one side to the other in a criss-cross fashion, to add an extra special touch.

PLAITING PROBLEMS

Where a horse has been poorly clipped, or has had his mane badly pulled in the past, you may find he has short hairs that stick straight upwards along his crest. These can detract from the streamlined look you are trying to create, but you must never cut them off, or the problem will be twice as bad the next time you come to plait. While these hairs are growing out you can use human hair gel to stick them down, without detriment to your horse's mane or appearance as it doesn't show.

There is no doubt that plaited tails look very elegant in the show ring – that is, as long as they are done properly. They are quite usual when showing youngstock, but are seen less on older show horses, especially those exhibited in mainstream showing classes such as hunters, cobs, riding horses and even hacks, who mostly have pulled tails. This is largely due to convenience, but also because a pulled tail looks more 'workmanlike'. However, a nicely plaited tail will always look better than a badly pulled one, and vice versa: at the end of the day it all comes down to personal preference and how well you can do the job! There is nothing worse than seeing a lovely horse in the show ring being let down by a plaited tail that is slowly escaping from the top downwards, and will end up resembling a bale of hay which has burst from its strings.

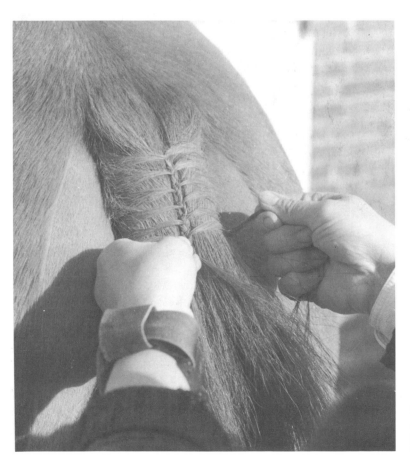

Plaiting a tail does take practice and it is easier if you have a good length to the hairs at the top of the tail.

Plaiting a tail does take practice, but it is easier if you have a good length to the top hairs of the tail to start with. If the tail has been pulled within the previous year you may find the task a hard one. The hardest bit is at the beginning, because you have to ensure that all the top hairs are well secured into the start of the plait – and unfortunately, these are always the shortest hairs. The reason many people have difficulty in plaiting a tail is because they start off by taking in too much hair at the start of the plait, or else they fail to keep everything tight as they work their way down; so be mindful of this when doing it yourself.

STEP-BY-STEP TAIL PLAITING TECHNIQUES

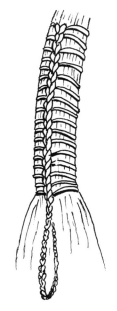

A ridged tail plait.

1.   Take hold of a *small* section of the uppermost hairs from each side of the dock and pull them taut.
2.   Next, select a similar sized section from the middle top hairs of the tail, so you have three individual sections of tail hair.
3.   There are two ways of plaiting a tail. Either you can have the plait lying *on top* of the tail (which is known as a ridge plait, *see* illustration) so that it has a raised appearance, in which case you pass the sections *underneath* each other as you plait; or you can have the plait lying *underneath* the hair so that it has a flat appearance, in which case you pass the sections of hair *on top* of each other.
4.   Plait down in exactly the same manner as was described for French plaiting a forelock, *see* the section on Plaiting Manes.
5.   Continue plaiting sections in from the side until you reach about two-thirds of the way down the dock, by which time you will be using the long hairs of the tail.
6.   With the hair that you have accumulated into the plait, but not taking in any more hair, keep plaiting down so that you end up with one long plaited strand.
7.   When you can plait no further, stitch up the end to prevent the hairs from unravelling.
8.   Make a loop of the last straggling hairs, and wind the thread around this to anchor the plait.
9.   With the needle and thread still attached, pass the needle up through the middle of the plait, at the point where you stopped taking hairs in from the sides (about two-thirds down the dock). This makes a long loop.
10.   Stitch up through the loop to bring both sides together. This ensures the plait lies straight and flat against the tail. Secure it all

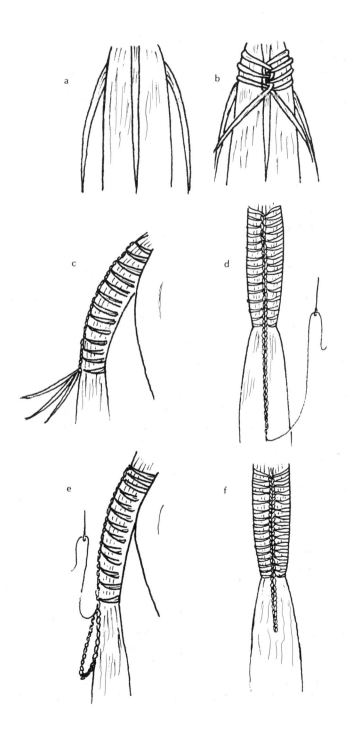

(a) Dividing the three strands;
(b) keeping the strands equal and
tight; (c) finishing the tail, and
starting to plait down;
(d) securing the bottom;
(e) making the loop; (f) how the
tail looks once finished.

Continue plaiting down so that you end up with one long strand.

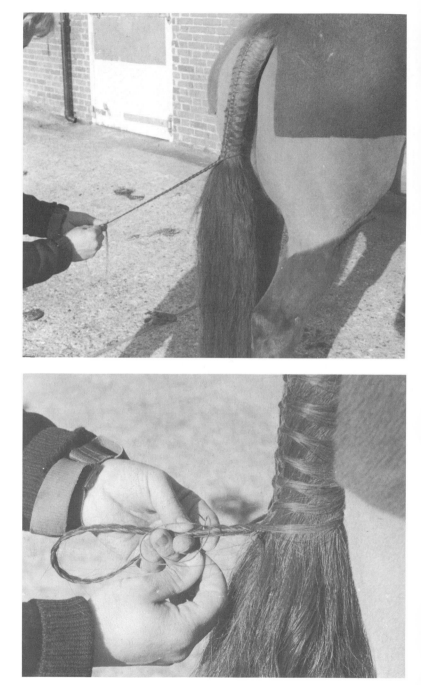

Pass the needle up through the middle of the plait, at the point where you stopped taking in hairs from the side.

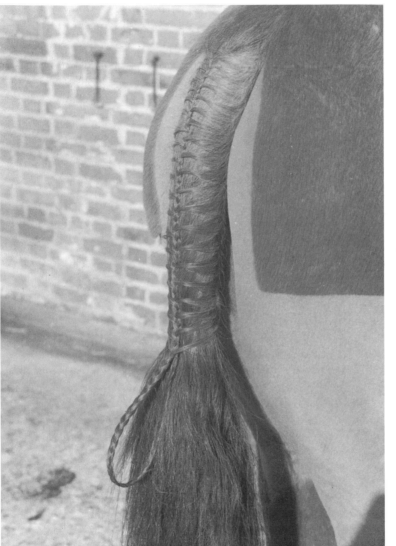

Make a loop with this long strand.

really well by winding the thread around the base of the top section to finish off.

11.   Once finished, do *not* be tempted to pluck out any loose hairs as this will just make it harder to plait next time. If they stick out and you are plaiting for a show, you can use some hair gel to make them lie flat until they have grown enough to be able to plait them in.

Stitch both sides of the loop
together so that it lies flat.

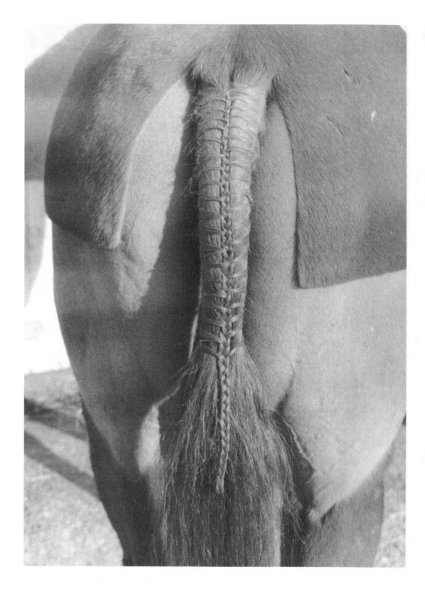

12.   It can be extremely annoying to leave home with a lovely
plaited tail only to arrive at the show with one that has been rubbed
and pulled out. This can happen when horses lean on their tails for
stability when travelling in a horsebox. Prevent this by either
bandaging all the way down the tail or by using a tail guard that fully
surrounds the whole tail.

APPLYING A TAIL BANDAGE

Unroll about 2–3in (5–7cm) of the bandage and then hold the loose end on to the very top of the tail so that it is facing upwards over the back. Wind the bandage around the very top of the tail, trying to ensure that all loose hairs are tucked in, until you have completed one whole turn. Then flap the free end down so that it will be covered the next time the bandage is coiled around the tail. This prevents the bandage from working loose and coming undone at the top. Carry on down the tail, covering just over half of the width of the bandage on each turn. It is important to achieve an even pressure all the way down: not so tight that it will restrict the horse's circulation and not so loose that it will slip off. When you reach the bottom of the dock start to work your way back up the tail again. The aim is to finish about 1in (2.5cm) from the top of the bandage. Take the tapes around the tail once (or twice if they are exceptionally long) ensuring you secure them with a bow on the *topside* of the tail. The tapes must not be left hanging loose, which could leave them open to be pulled or rubbed undone. There are various ways of preventing this. If the bandage is intended to lay the tail flat for grooming then you can simply fold the turn of the bandage immediately above the tapes down over them. If you are going to travel the horse in a box it is sensible to protect them securely, either by using tape (which is very sticky) or by sewing them.

To remove a tail bandage, do not unravel it all. Simply undo the tapes and slide it off downwards. This helps to make the tail lie flat, creating a good appearance.

QUARTER MARKS

A neatly plaited or pulled tail can set off the quarters very well, and if these are enhanced by sharks' teeth or quarter marks, the horse will really stand out in the crowd. 'Sharks' teeth' are triangular-shaped brush marks, with the thin end pointing towards the stifle, and so-called because they look like sharks' teeth! Quarter marks can be made in two ways: either a ready-made plastic pattern with the squares already cut out can be used – lay it over the horse's coat and then brush against the lie of the hair; remove the pattern and you are left with alternate squares, the hair that has been brushed making an attractive chess-board pattern. You can make the same marks by using a 1in (2.5cm) piece of mane comb. Use the comb against the lie of the coat to form a 1in (2.5cm) square, then miss a square, then repeat, working in a chess-board fashion. This method does take a little more practice, but it has the advantage over the pre-cut patterns as you can tailor the shape to suit your own horse.

Common quarter marks.

The main reason for clipping horses is to prevent them from sweating excessively in the winter months, which they would do if worked hard in a full winter coat. A clipped horse may still sweat, of course, but he will be far less likely to catch a chill as he will dry more quickly. Always remember that a clipped horse must have his lost coat replaced with suitable rugs, both in the stable and field and sometimes when exercised.

Where you begin clipping is largely a matter of personal choice. However, it is often a good idea to start with the head, especially if the horse gets fidgety as time goes on, as he will not have had the chance to have got fed up and bored so soon – a situation which always makes a fidgety horse worse. However, if you are not used to clipping you might prefer to start along his neck so as to get used to the feel of the clippers before tackling any tricky bits. And if the *horse* is not used to clippers, it is best to start along his shoulder in the first instance, so that he is not startled by the feel or sound of them around his head.

Start by just resting the clippers against him while they are not turned on; then move them over his body while they are still switched off so that he gets used to the look of them and the cable. Next, take them some way away from him and switch them on; leave them running for a few minutes so he can become accustomed to the noise. Gradually walk towards him, stopping if he seems alarmed. Approach at a pace that suits him, reassuring him all the time, before you finally put them against his coat. Again, move them all over his body, but without actually clipping any hairs off. It may take a few days before you are able to clip the horse properly, but if you do take such measures to introduce the clippers in this way, he will never become scared of being clipped.

Make sure you have a brush and oil ready in order to prepare the clippers for use, a straw bale to stand on, and a helper on hand should you need assistance to keep the horse still. Before a horse can be clipped he should have been thoroughly groomed to remove any dirt and grease from his coat. Then put on a tail bandage to prevent the tail from getting in the way when you do the quarters. If your horse's mane does not lie flat you might also want to plait this over to prevent it getting in the way of the blades.

TYPES OF CLIPPERS

There are four basic types of clippers in use. The first and most com-

---

TIP

Attach hand-held clippers to a wrist strap so that if they accidentally slip out of your hand they will not come to any harm nor frighten your horse. Electric clippers can sustain a fair amount of damage if they are dropped on to a hard surface.

mon are **electric clippers,** which plug into a mains socket; they should always be connected to a circuit breaker so they will switch off in the event of an emergency. This type of clippers you simply hold with one hand, while keeping the electrical cable out the way behind you.

The second type are **heavy duty** clippers, generally used in large establishments where there are many horses to clip. These are often suspended on a pulley or rail from the ceiling or a beam, a system which allows you to clip a horse without fear of his treading on, or becoming entangled in the cable.

The third type are easier to handle as they are **battery-operated**. They work from a battery pack which is strapped to your back, so you can work unhindered by any cables, and they are undoubtedly the safest type of clippers in use.

Heavy duty electric clippers.

Battery-operated clippers are undoubtedly the safest.

The last type are small **trimming models**, used for small areas only rather than for clipping a whole horse; for example they can be useful for clipping the head of a headshy horse as they are usually very quiet.

When selecting any set of clippers, try to select those which are quiet running and smooth in operation.

TYPES OF CLIP

The clip you decide to give your horse will depend on how he is kept and the work he does. The aim is to remove as little hair as is necessary: you need to prevent him from sweating excessively, but you also need to keep him warm. While you can rug him up well and offer him extra feed to maintain condition and prevent heat loss, neither of these makes up completely for the loss of the natural coat. Take a look at the following descriptions to give you a rough guide as to what might suit your horse best.

Full Total removal of all the coat: mostly used on horses in hard work, such as hunters and eventers. It is unwise to give your horse a full clip unless he is in competitive, hard work. No leg protection is offered, so horses with full clips should not be exercised without boots or bandages. This is highly impractical for most animals, as there is a high risk of becoming cold, and chilling.

Hunter Removal of all coat except legs and saddle patch: for horses in hard work where leg and back protection is desirable, such as hunting. This is a variation on the full clip, offering more defence against the elements by leaving the hair on the legs, though the loins are still uncovered.

Blanket The coat is left on the legs, and from wither to tail, extending half way down the horse's sides: for stabled horses in medium work where warmth over the loins is required. This is a useful clip for cold-blooded horses, as the loins, and therefore the kidneys, are kept warm. Horses can be turned out if fully rugged.

Chaser Similar to a blanket clip, but the coat extends up the neck to the bridle patch to keep the main galloping muscles warm. Used on horses in medium work, this is a practical clip, keeping the quarters covered. Horses can be turned out if fully rugged.

Trace Similar to the chaser clip but the coat is left on over the front part of the head, and the 'blanket' is lower: for rugged horses at grass or ones only stabled at night. It follows the trace lines of a carriage

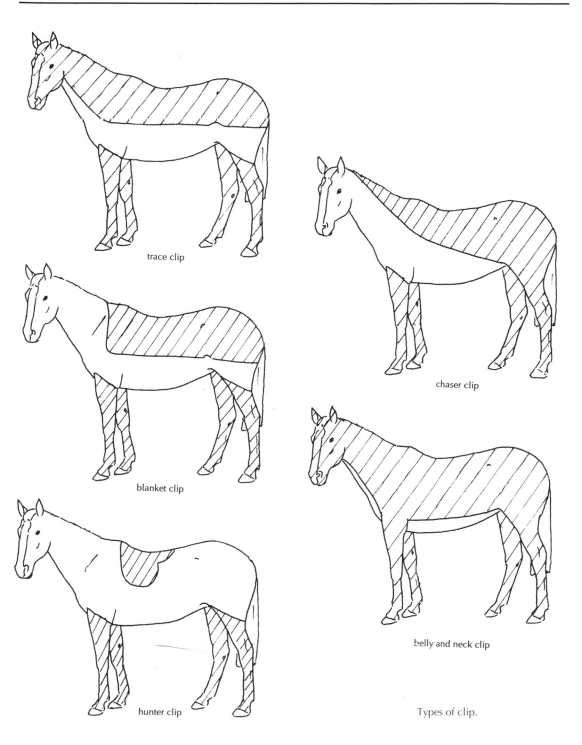

trace clip

chaser clip

blanket clip

belly and neck clip

hunter clip

Types of clip.

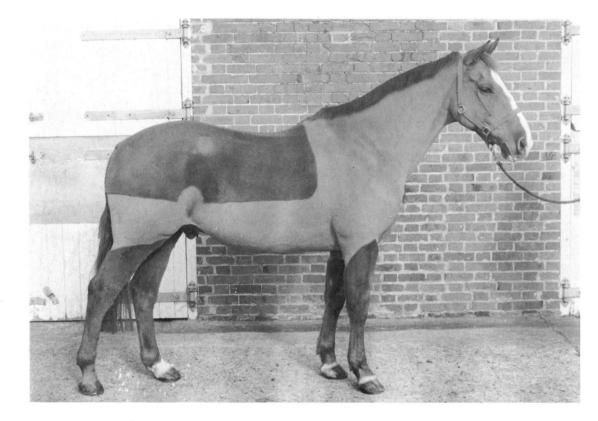

A neat blanket clip which provides warmth over the loins.

harness, and is very practical for horses in light work. Useful for nervous horses, as the hair on the ears and sensitive facial areas is left on.

Neck and Belly   Just a small section under the neck and belly is removed. Most commonly used on horses in light work, and animals kept at grass. Also known as a 'sweat clip', as just the areas most prone to sweating are removed.

EQUIPMENT CHECKLIST

Clippers   Spare blades, lubricating oil, brush and cloth to remove hairs and grease, chalk or saddle soap to mark lines, circuit breaker for power source.

Person clipping and assistant   Protective overalls, hard hat, rubber-soled shoes.

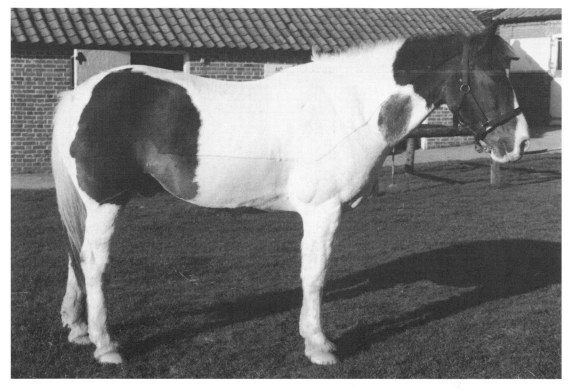

Horse Safe head collar and lead rope, rugs, haynet to keep occupied.
Additional Appropriate sedation (arrange beforehand), twitch, bridle or chifney (anti-rearing bit), secure object to stand on, broom and shovel to clear up hair.
Conditions Good lighting, flat, non-slip surface, dry weather if outside, plenty of time available.

A trace clip is ideal for horses that are out at grass in the day and stabled at night, and are only in light work.

PREPARING TO CLIP

Before you start to clip, make sure your blades are sharp and clean. It is also a good idea to have a spare, sharpened pair standing by, as grease from the coat can soon blunt a pair of blades. Run a little oil along them, and put some in the appropriate holes (refer to the manufacturer's instructions for your particular model); this will keep them running smoothly and clipping efficiently.

CLIPPING TIPS

• Wear overalls or old clothes, as clipping is a very messy business. The hair will work its way right into your clothes and is extremely difficult to remove.
• Aim to make the outline of the clip straight and even. To help you, clip these lines while the horse is relaxed, leaving the larger, less tricky areas until later.
• Start clipping in the morning so you can finish the clip in the same day that you start.
• Wear rubber-soled boots for insulation against electrical faults.
• Long, smooth strokes ensure a sleeker, less 'tram-lined' finish.
• Always keep the clippers flat against the skin, pushing them against the lie of the coat.
• Be guided by the lie of the coat; when it changes direction, so should the clippers.
• Smooth out any wrinkles before clipping, either with your spare hand, or by having an assistant hold up a leg, or the head as appropriate.
• Check the heat of the blades regularly, allowing time for them to cool if they are heating up, before recommencing clipping.
• Oil the blades regularly.

Make sure you have your horse in a brightly lit area that is away from draughts, and have a blanket ready in case he starts to feel the cold. You can then put the blanket over his quarters while clipping the forehand, and over his withers and loins while clipping his quarters. This is not often necessary, but you must be prepared.

Consider the surface your horse will be standing on, too; while it may be more convenient for you if your horse is standing on a bare floor, it may not be as safe or comfortable for him. Rubber flooring is the ideal as it also protects against electric shocks, but as yet this is not a common flooring. If you intend to clip in a stable make sure there is a thin layer of straw on the floor. This will provide a certain amount of grip for the horse should he shuffle and fidget, and will also allow him to stale should he wish to do so.

You should have decided on the type of clip you wish to give your horse long before the day of clipping, because you need to prepare him for the type of clip he is going to have. To do this you can mark the outline with chalk, or saddle soap. If the horse is having a hunter clip, put on his usual saddle and chalk an outline around this, to ensure you get an even shape on both sides.

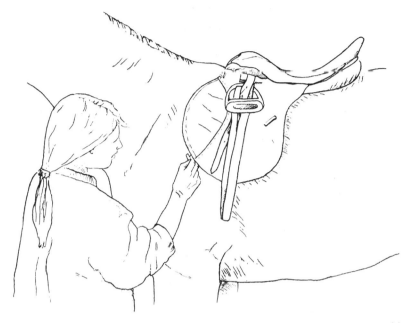

Marking around the saddle with chalk, for a hunter clip.

STEP-BY-STEP CLIPPING TECHNIQUES

Having prepared the clippers, the horse and the working area, tie up the horse, or have someone hold him if he seems a little apprehensive. Turn on the clippers and allow him to become accustomed to their sound before placing them on him, even if he has been clipped many times before. Work on him in areas, getting the tricky bits out of the way first. There is no way of telling how long it will take you to clip a horse: it all depends on the type of clip, the temperament of the horse, and how experienced you are at clipping. An experienced person may take only an hour to give a well behaved horse a hunter clip. For a less experienced person or a badly behaved horse it may take all day, so always allow yourself plenty of time.

The Neck

Always run the clippers against the lie of the coat. When clipping near the mane you need a steady hand; don't go too close, as you will be in danger of removing the mane hairs, which will then grow back stiff and upright like a Mohican hairstyle. Try to use one long

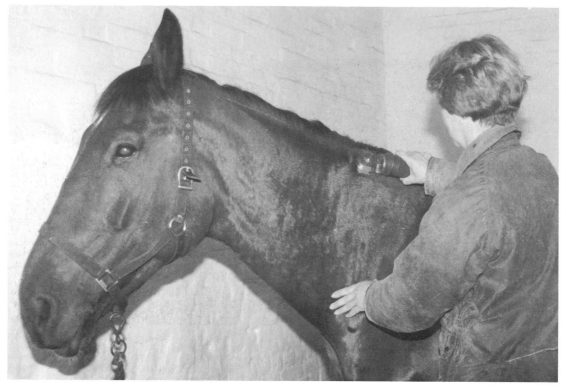

When clipping near the mane
you need a steady hand.

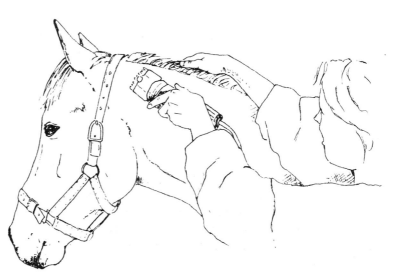

Make sure you do not clip into
the mane.

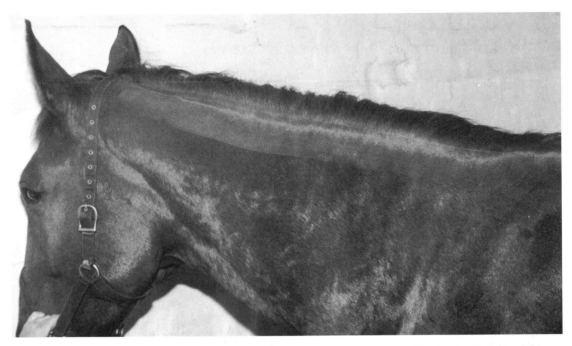

movement, allowing the blades to glide naturally through the coat, rather than pushing them; this will help you to get a nice straight line.

Allowing the blades to glide through the coat, rather than pushing them through, will ensure a straight line.

The Head

When clipping the head, make sure you place a hand over your horse's eye while you clip away any hair above. It is quite difficult to clip around the eyes, so don't worry too much if you cannot get into all the little crevices; the hair here is often very short and will soon blend in after a short time.

The Ears

Some horses dislike the sound of the clippers around their ears, so go carefully. Some people pad their horses' ears with cotton wool, but I would not recommend this: first, some may be left inside after removal, and in any case it is the vibration, rather than the sound which horses seem to dislike. Pull the ears forwards and, starting at the base, clip over it from side to side. Then run the clippers from the tip of the ear, right down to the base.

When clipping the head, make sure you place your hand over your horse's eye as you clip the hairs above it.

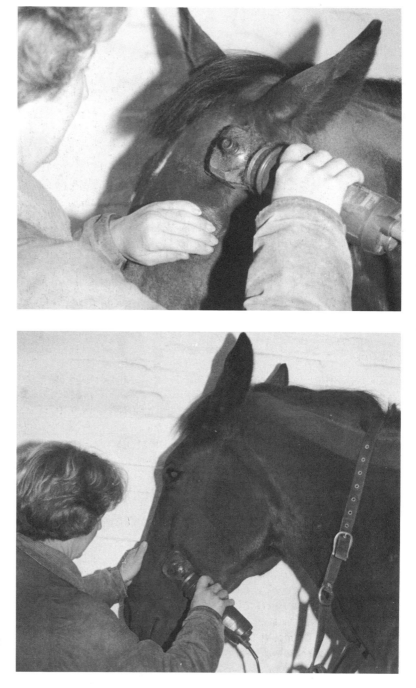

Don't worry too much if you cannot get into all the little crevices, as this hair is very short and often blends in unnoticeably.

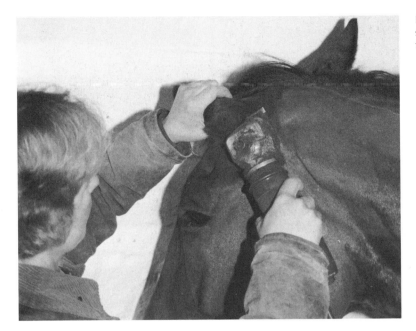

Pull the ear forwards and, starting at the base, clip over it from one side to the other.

The Tail

At the tail it is much more professional to make a point, leaving the coat hair as a triangle, rather than simply clipping straight across which is often done, but looks ghastly. Initially clip wider than the shape you eventually intend to make: run the clippers from the top of the tail on one side obliquely to a point right in the centre of your horse's backbone; repeat this on the other side, finishing at the same spot on the backbone thus making the 'point' of the triangle. Then trim slightly closer if necessary to get a straight line and an even triangle shape.

The Hind Legs

Starting at the rear of the hind legs, clip forwards, making a diagonal line which follows the direction of the gaskin (second thigh). To judge this, hold your thumb on the stifle and where your middle finger comes is about the place where the top of the clip line should be. Then clip a symmetrical diagonal line on the inside of the thigh, forming a 'V' on the back tendon above and in line with the hocks. To judge where the point of the 'V' should be, put your middle finger

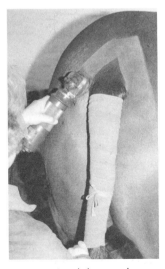

Leave a pointed shape at the top of the tail, rather than simply cutting straight across.

(a) Marking the top (a) and bottom (b) of the diagonal hind leg clip line.

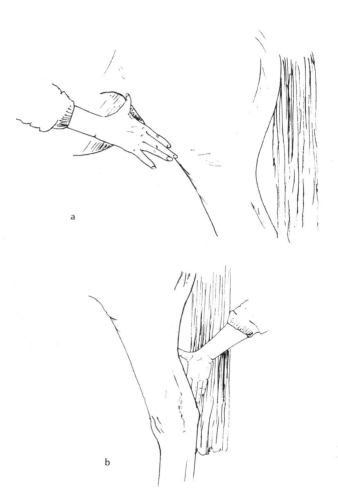

a

b

about 1in (2.5cm) above the hock and stretch your thumb up the back of the leg; where your thumb comes to rest should be about the lowest point of the 'V', that is, the clip line (*see* illustrations).

The Stifle

This can be a tricky area to clip as most horses are ticklish here. Put your hand behind the stifle and pull it out so that you have a flat surface to work on. Remove all the hair, first working from the quarters into the centre of the stifle, and then from the belly to the centre.

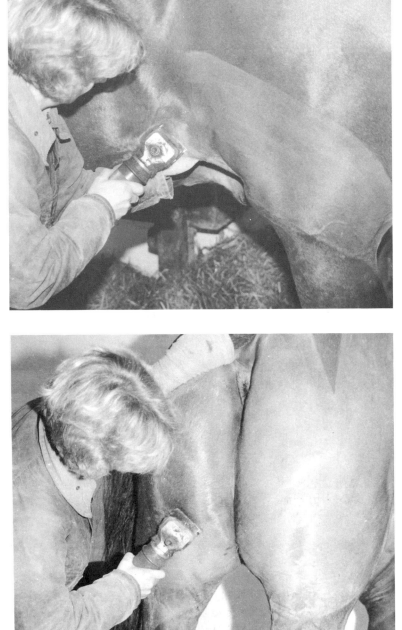

Put your hand behind the stifle and pull it out so that you have a flat surface to clip.

Be careful to stand to the side when clipping the rear of the hindquarters.

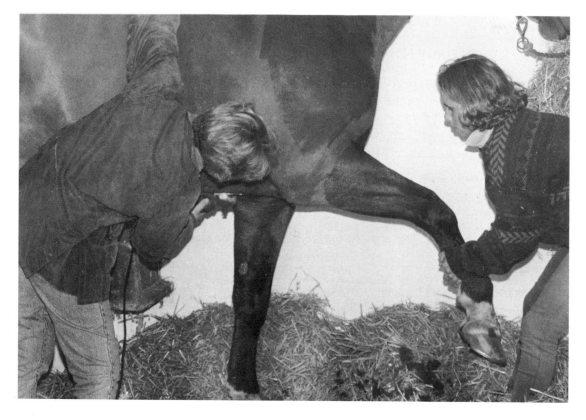

To clip round the elbows, have someone hold the horse's leg forwards.

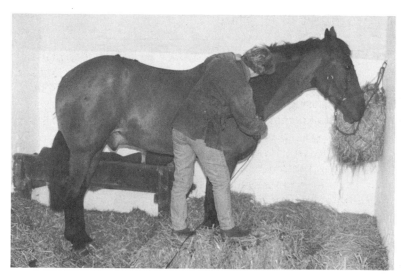

For high areas use a straw bale to stand on

The Front Legs

The line of clip on the front leg should also run diagonally from rear to front, starting about 2in (5cm) below the point of elbow. Clip quite high at first, so you can run back along the line if needs be, to straighten it. However, do not keep on fiddling with these lines, or you will end up somewhere near the knee!

Folds

When clipping away hair from places where the skin folds, try to stretch the skin so that you can clip on a flat, straight surface. To be able to do this around the elbows, you will have to ask someone to hold the leg forwards.

Big Areas

Large areas of hair should be taken a section at a time, although try to keep an even contact between the clippers and the coat, otherwise you will end up with streaks. For high areas, use your straw bale to stand on.

Once finished, give your horse a quick brush off to remove the loose hair, then quickly rug him up because he will feel cold without his natural protection.

METHODS OF RESTRAINT

Unfortunately, many horses do not like being clipped, perhaps because of bad experiences in the past, or just because they are being pigheaded. Either way you have to deal with the situation as best you can, using whatever method of restraint might be appropriate. The most common of these is the twitch, a cord which is put around the upper lip of the horse and twisted until tight. It works because the pressure for some reason causes the brain to release an endorphin-like substance which acts as a natural pain relief and calmative. Other methods range from simply holding up a leg to prevent the horse from moving, to having the vet sedate the horse.

All these methods can become very annoying, however, and each has its own drawback: the twitch needs to be removed frequently, and then the horse may be less than enthusiastic about having it put back on; holding up a leg requires the help of another person, and

---

WHEN TO CLIP

Most horses have grown their winter coats by early to mid-autumn so this is the time to clip if your horse is in work. If the horse has been well rugged up in late summer he may be encouraged to grow a finer coat, thus preventing the need for clipping altogether, or at least making the job far easier. If the horse is only doing light work, you may get away with not clipping at all.

Once clipped, a horse will probably need reclipping about three times during the winter months, with the last clip being done at the end of January, and certainly no later than the end of February; by this time he will be starting to grow his summer coat.

A twitch is a common form of restraint when clipping.

can be back-breaking; sedating the horse costs money, and so on. It is obvious, then, that the best solution is to get the horse used to the clippers in such a way that they will never hold any fear for him; even if the process takes a month, it will be well worth the effort in years to come.

Do not let all this put you off. Many horses don't trouble themselves at all about being clipped: they just doze, and lap up all the attention they are being given.

MAINTENANCE OF YOUR CLIPPERS

Keeping your clippers in good repair all year round is essential – look after them, and when you come to use them there will be no panic about sharpening or repairing. Arrange for your clippers to be sharpened earlier on in the year, so they are in good working order by September. When in use, keep the blades as clean as possible, brushing regularly with a stiff brush. Lubricate with grease or 3-in-1 oil; clipper manufacturers will advise you on which oil is bet for your make of clippers. Do ont allow them to overheat while you are clipping – stop and let them cool down for a while, making sure your horse is kept warm. Always take the clippers apart after use and clean each part thoroughly. Though this may be time consuming, in the long run it will be beneficial, as repairs can be expensive. Make sure you carry a spare set of blades with you when you are clipping, in case the first set becomes too blunt.

CLIPPING FOR VETERINARY PURPOSES

In some cases you may need to clip your horse for practical hygiene reasons, as a result of a disease or wound. For instance, mud fever, a condition where the leg is encrusted with scabs as a result of water-logged or muddy legs, may require the affected area to be clipped. Heavier horses with thicker leg hair and feathers are most likely to require this treatment. The hair holds in moisture, so when the leg is bathed it does not dry properly. Any ointments and treatments will therefore not reach the desired area, creating a mass of sticky, damp hair. As damp hair carries and holds bacteria, clipping the affected area will not only keep the leg dry but enable you to carry out hygiene treatment successfully as well.

Method

Take great care when clipping the leg, as you will need to get close to the ground. Remember that your horse will be uncomfortable, and may try to kick out at you; it is safer to have an assistant to hold the leg you are not clipping. The discomfort a horse feels when you remove a scab will be multiplied when you clip a sore area, so be careful and gentle. Smaller, battery-operated clippers will be easier to manoeuvre, though if the hair is very thick they may take too long. Always apply a barrier cream on to a dry, clipped leg to prevent the condition worsening.

Sometimes the area surrounding a wound may need clipping or trimming, though only on veterinary advice. If your horse has a thick winter coat and a weeping wound, the area will be difficult to treat, and may hamper recovery. In this situation, heavy-duty electric clippers may be too cumbersome, so battery clippers are best. Take care not to touch the wound, just remove the surrounding hair. Consult a veterinary expert if you are in any doubt.

SUMMER CLIPPING

Clipping during the spring and summer months is usually only

A full clip with legs left on.

necessary for competition horses. Unless your horse has a very thick summer coat and does a lot of regular, hard work, you will not need to clip throughout the year. There are two reasons for summer clipping; the first is practical. A competition horse will need to sweat freely and recover quickly, and even a thin layer of extra coat can hinder this. Also, grooming and presentation will be made easier if the coat is cleaner – a clipped horse on a sunny day will dry very quickly when bathed. Any dirt can be swiftly removed by grooming, making the show/competition preparation quicker and more convenient. The second reason is to enhance the horse's appearance, especially in showing classes. Careful clipping can improve the profile of a show horse or cob, and can even improve the depth of colour of some horses.

AFTER-CARE OF THE CLIPPED HORSE

Your horse will take a while to adjust to his new clip, and likewise his body temperature should be allowed to stabilize. He should be rugged up at all times, though the number of rugs you give him should correspond with his type and breed. For instance, a thin-skinned thoroughbred would need thicker rugs than a native breed, though too many rugs can cause overheating, sweating and possibly dehydration. Woollen rugs can be very abrasive on sensitive clipped skin, so make sure the bottom layer is comfortable – a cotton sheet underneath the rug or blanket will not irritate, and is also easy to wash, saving the rug from getting too dirty. When turned out your horse will need a thick New Zealand or waterproof turnout rug, and maybe an under rug when the weather is really cold.

You will find lots of loose hairs and grease in your horse's coat after he has been clipped. A thorough grooming with a soft brush and a damp cloth will work wonders – bathing is not advisable unless the weather is very warm or you have proper drying facilities.

EXERCISING/COOLING OFF THE CLIPPED HORSE

It is of prime importance when you are exercising or schooling to keep your horse warm. A lined, waterproof exercise sheet should do the trick, though if he does get wet, keep him moving so the blood circulation regulates his body temperature. On return to the stable, dry him thoroughly and use a sweat rug or an upside-down jute rug to wick the moisture off his skin. Thatching your horse with straw under his rug is very effective, though check him periodically to make sure the straw has not slipped down. If you are lucky enough to be riding indoors, keep a rug over his quarters until he has phys-ically warmed up, and be sure to put it back on as you are winding down the work so your horse doesn't chill. You may find various pads and numnahs such as sheepskin are useful, as they promote heat, keeping the back muscles warm and supple.

CLIPPING PROFESSIONALS

You may be lucky enough to possess your own clippers, though many owners with one or two horses find the initial outlay too expensive. When you add to the clippers' cost keep and mainte-nance, including new blades and re-sharpening, you may find it cheaper to hire a professional to clip your horse. Clipping services

A horse in hard work will probably need either a hunter or full clip.

are often advertised in saddlers' and tack shops, and in the equestrian press. Personal recommendation is always helpful, so ask equestrian friends who they have to clip their horses. Some people may specialize in difficult horses or in particular types of clip, so ask around and compare services. Different clippers may charge by the hour, by the type of clip or size of horse, and some include petrol in their charge. Make sure you know the cost of the service before you have someone out to clip your horse, as unexpected charges will be unwelcome! An experienced horse clipper will be able to advise on what type of clip would suit you and your horse, so have a chat first and explain your situation. Your clipper may need to plan his schedule around you, and will need to estimate how long it will take. It is very important to be totally honest about your horse. It is no use saying 'he is a little ticklish' if he turns into a quivering wreck when approached with a set of clippers. Anyone who advertises their services knows they will encounter difficult horses, so tell them how your horse is likely to react, and how many times he has been clipped before. Any veterinary treatment such as sedation will need to be pre-booked, and your feeding schedule and your clipping appointment should be arranged accordingly.